laurie polich short

STUDIES ON THE GO

MATTHEW

ZONDERVAN®   youth specialties

ZONDERVAN

Matthew
Copyright © 2014 by Laurie Short

YS Youth Specialties is a trademark of Real Resources Incorporated and is registered with the United States Patent and Trademark Office.

This title is also available as a Zondervan ebook.
Visit www.zondervan.com/ebooks.

Requests for information should be addressed to:

Zondervan, 3900 *Sparks Dr. SE, Grand Rapids, Michigan 49546*

Library of Congress Cataloging-in-Publication Data

Polich Short, Laurie.
    Matthew / Laurie Polich Short.
        pages cm. — (Studies on the go)
    ISBN 978-0-310-51675-0 (softcover)
    1. Bible. Matthew — Study and teaching. 2. Church work with youth. I. Title.
BS2576.P65 2014
226.20071'2 — dc22
                                                                2014026651

Cover design: Toolbox Studios
Interior design: SharpSeven Design/David Conn

Printed in the United States of America

14 15 16 17 18 19 20 /DCI/ 22 21 20 19 18 17 16 15 14 13 12 11 10 9 8 7 6 5 4 3 2 1

DEDICATION AND ACKNOWLEDGMENTS

To youth workers young and old —you are my heroes! And to the legacy of Youth Specialties — you will always hold a place in my heart.

Special thanks to:

— Dave Urbanski and Ryan Pazdur who helped bring another Studies on the Go into print.

— Zondervan publishers who did this book and graciously gave me the opportunity to broaden my ministry with *Finding Faith in the Dark.*

— Jon Ireland and Jono Shaffer, former youth ministers who serve with me at Ocean Hills — now that my stepson is a preteen, I am thankful he has a great church community. It takes a village!

CONTENTS

HOW TO USE STUDIES ON THE GO

Welcome to a look inside the book of Matthew. It is my prayer that you and your students discover a treasure chest in this first Gospel account of Jesus' life. There are jewels in Matthew—including the Beatitudes, the Sermon on the Mount, and The Great Commission—that we find in no other Gospel. The texts are rich and colorful, and they include more detail than we find in the accounts from Mark, Luke, and John. It is well worth your time to study this book with your students. My job is to make it engaging and fun.

I must confess after writing four of these studies that we may have misnamed this series. These are not "drive by" Bible studies, aimed only at skimming the surface. These are rich, deep studies aimed at providing the busy youth worker with a tool he or she can trust.

As I've said before with Studies on the Go, feel free to pick and choose the questions that best suit your group. Each study contains 15 questions and an optional activity, which will probably be too much for a single session. I suggest you take your time with the questions that unlock something in your students and skip the ones that don't. You know your students, and depending on their age and spiritual maturity, you can best make the call on the questions you need.

There are three kinds of questions in this book: **Observation** questions which take you to the text, **Interpretation** questions which help you think about the text, and **Application** questions which help your students live the text.

Unless God's Word takes root in our lives, our study is fruitless. Therefore my suggestion is you spend 10 minutes observing, 20 minutes interpreting, and 25 minutes applying (which can include the optional activity at the end of each session). That leaves 5-10 min at the beginning of your study for your intro question, which you can select from the three options at the top of the page.

Have fun! And I always like to remind small group leaders that Jesus did some of his best work through questions. Let that fuel your fire as you begin these studies with your students.

Enjoy your journey through Matthew!

P.S. If you like this book, be sure to also check out my other studies in John, Romans, and Genesis. And if you need some basic tools for leading a small group, try *Help! I'm a Small Group Leader.*

1. CHOSEN BY GOD
Matthew 1

LEADER'S INSIGHT

Imagine being able to trace your ancestors back to the beginning of time.

That's what Matthew 1 does for Jesus. Most of us are lucky if we know our great-grandparents. Jesus knew his great, great, great . . . (I'd better stop here; I don't have enough space for the number of greats I need.) If you look closely, you can see that Matthew does it for a purpose. Old Testament prophecy was fulfilled through Jesus' lineage.

In Matthew 1, we see that Joseph was handpicked to be Jesus' earthly father. Though his seed wasn't in Jesus, his family was the context through which Jesus came. It was Joseph who made Jesus' lineage so special.

Sometimes we brush over genealogies because they seem boring. But don't miss the details of this one with your students. To see Abraham at the beginning, giving Jesus his Jewish roots. To see King David in the middle, revealing the royalty from which he came. To notice that all five women in the lineup have stories of amazing grace, showing God can take the mess of our lives and do great things if we let him.

Genealogies carry important details that reveal insights about who we are. This genealogy carries important details about who God is— and how he came in the person of Jesus.

Share

- If God came to you in a dream and gave you a plan for your life that was different than yours, would you follow it?

- What do you know about your genealogy? Is there anything you know about your parents or grandparents that tells you more about who you are?

- How much of your life do you think is preplanned? How much do you think happens by choice?

Observe

Observation Questions

- Where does the genealogy begin in Matthew 1? Whose name is at the end, before Jesus? How many generations are represented? (See verse 17.)

- What did Joseph have in mind when he found out Mary was pregnant?

- How did God come to Joseph? What did God say? What Old Testament verse is referenced in verse 23?

- What did Joseph do after God spoke to him? Did he have union with his wife before Jesus was born?

Think

Interpretation Questions

- Do you think Joseph was preplanned to be Jesus' earthly father? Why/Why not?

- What does verse 19 tell you about the kind of man Joseph was? Do you think he was cruel or kind?

- How do verses 22-23 show God's providence in this situation? Do you think Mary and Joseph had a choice regarding how they responded to God?

- What does verse 24 say about Joseph's faith? What does verse 25 reveal about Jesus' birth? Based on this verse, what kind of father was Joseph to Jesus?

Apply

Application Questions

- How far back can you trace your genealogy? Is there anyone in your genealogy who is famous for something?

- If you were Joseph, do you think you would have done what the Lord told him to do? Why/Why not?

- On a scale of 1-10, how much faith do you think Joseph had? (1=no faith, 10=a lot of faith). Where would you put yourself on that scale?

- What is one dream you have for your life? Have you ever had a dream you felt God wanted you to do?

Do

Optional Activity

Have your students write out their genealogies as far as they know them. Then, over the next week, have them trace their genealogies as far back as they are able—by interviewing their parents, grandparents, great-grandparents, etc., to find out all the information they can. Have them come back to the group next week with one fact about their genealogies that surprises them, a person in their genealogies who inspires them, and a quality they have inherited from someone they admire.

QUIET TIME REFLECTIONS

Day 1: Matthew 1:1-5

- What word or verse stands out to you from this passage? Why?

- Who were the three women in this part of the genealogy? What do you know about their stories? (See Genesis 38, Joshua 2, Ruth 1.)

- Spend time today thinking about how God can make our story part of his story when we give our life to him.

Day 2: Matthew 1:6-11

- What word or verse stands out to you from this passage? Why?

- Why do you think Bathsheba is listed as Uriah's wife rather than David's? (See 2 Samuel 11.) What does that tell you about how God remembers us?

- Spend time today thinking about how God honors us when we do the right thing even when we get hurt by it.

Day 3: Matthew 1:12-17

- What word or verse stands out to you from this passage? Why?

- Whose line did Jesus' genealogy come through, Mary or Joseph? What does that tell you about the importance of Joseph in Mary's selection as the mother of Jesus?

- Spend time thinking about how God is concerned with every detail of our lives and has a plan for each one of us!

Day 4: Matthew 1:18-19

- What word or phrase stands out to you from these verses? Why?

- What does Joseph's response to Mary's pregnancy tell you about the kind of man he was?

- Spend time thinking today about how you would respond to circumstances that were not what you wanted.

Day 5: Matthew 1:20-21

- What word or phrase stands out to you from these verses? Why?

- What did the angel tell Joseph to do? How do you think he felt when he heard this?

- Spend time thinking about what you would do if God told you to do something way outside your comfort zone.

Day 6: Matthew 1:22-25

- What word or verse stands out to you from this passage? Why?

- What prophecy did Mary fulfill in this chapter? (See Isaiah 7:14.) What was Jesus going to be called?

- Spend time thinking today about what it means that Jesus was Immanuel—God with us.

Day 7: Matthew 1

Read through the whole chapter and write out the verse that spoke to you most this week. Meditate on that verse today—and for an extra challenge, memorize it!

2. THE REAL KING
Matthew 2

LEADER'S INSIGHT

What makes a king a king?

Your students are familiar with the idea of monarchy from watching the royal family in Great Britain. A king (or queen) is different from a president. You cannot "run" for king; you can only be born one. That is true for both kings in Matthew 2.

The second chapter of Matthew contrasts two kings: Herod and Jesus. Both were born into their positions; however, one had a power that far exceeded the other. As the chapter goes on, your students will see which one was the real king.

When the Magi arrived from the east, the people of Jerusalem directed them to Herod. However, the stars were directing them somewhere else. Herod's discomfort at the birth of Jesus revealed who held the real power. We also see Jesus as the true king in the dreams threaded through this chapter. God used people's dreams to protect and position Jesus away from harm. There was a greater power at work than Herod's control.

In the end, Herod tried to stop Jesus by using his power in the most destructive way possible. Thousands of innocent young lives were lost, but Jesus wasn't one of them. Even as a baby, Jesus was above Herod's control, proving that he was the real king.

He still is.

Share

- When you think of a king, what is the first image that comes to your mind? In your opinion, who is the greatest historical king who ever lived?

- Have you ever studied the stars? What is the most unusual thing you've ever seen in the sky? (Shooting star? Comet? A certain shape or constellation?)

- If you were told in a dream to do something, do you think you would do it? Has that ever happened to you?

Observe

Observation Questions

- When did the Magi come to Jerusalem—at Jesus' birth, or after? Why did they come? Who did they go to see first?

- What did Herod find out about the child through the teachers of the law? (verses 5-6) What did he tell the Magi to do? (verse 8)

- What were the three gifts the Magi gave to the child? (verse 11) Why didn't they go back to Herod? (verse 12)

- How many dreams did Joseph have to direct his steps? (verses 13, 19-20) What did his first dream tell him to do? Where did Joseph end up?

Think

Interpretation Questions

- Why do you think it was a star that led the Magi to Jesus? What does that tell you about the significance of Jesus' birth?

- Why do you think all of Jerusalem was disturbed when King Herod was disturbed in verse 3? How do you think the people felt about him?

- How does the prophecy in verse 6 tie back to Jesus' gene-alogy and birth? (See Matthew 1:2-3.) What words in the prophecy validate Jesus as the coming Messiah?

- What does Herod's response in verse 16 tell you about the kind of king he was? What do Joseph's dreams in this chapter tell you about the power of Jesus' kingship over Herod's?

Apply

Application Questions

- If you saw a huge star (or something unusual) in the sky, what do you think you would do? Who would you tell about it?

- Have you ever felt like God was speaking to you about some-thing? If so, when? How do you discern when it is God's voice or something else?

- If people asked you what makes Jesus different from other religious leaders, what in this chapter could you refer to?

- Where do you look when you want God's guidance? When was the last time you felt he was leading you to do some-thing (or go somewhere)?

Do

Optional Activity

Have your students make a list of some of the great kings or presidents they remember through history, and what characteristics they think are important in a king. Then as a group, look at Matthew 2, and make a list of the character qualities you see in Herod. Give a grade to Herod as to what kind of king he was.

QUIET TIME REFLECTIONS

Day 1: Matthew 2:1-3

- What word or verse stands out to you from this passage? Why?

- What does Herod's response to the Magi tell you about the kind of king he was?

- Spend time today thinking about whether you are threatened when someone else gets attention.

Day 2: Matthew 2:4-8

- What word or verse stands out to you from this passage? Why?

- What prophecy was fulfilled by the place of Jesus' birth? (See Micah 5:2.)

- Spend time thinking today about God's sovereignty in the way Jesus fulfilled Old Testament prophecy even when he had no control over where he was.

Day 3: Matthew 2:9-12

- What word or verse stands out to you from this passage? Why?

- How were the Magi warned not to go back to Herod? What does that tell you about God's involvement in Jesus' life?

- Spend time thinking today about the way God guides you. Does he use other people? The Bible? Conviction?

Day 4: Matthew 2:13-15

- What word or verse stands out to you from this passage? Why?

- What prophecy was fulfilled by the guidance God gave Joseph? (See Hosea 11:1.)

- Spend time thinking today about how the small circumstances of our lives are all a part of a bigger picture.

Day 5: Matthew 2:16-18

- What word or verse stands out to you from this passage? Why?

- What prophecy was fulfilled by Herod's horrible actions? (See Jeremiah 31:15.) What does that show you about God?

- Spend time thinking today about how God knows our intentions and our hearts.

Day 6: Matthew 2:19-23

- What word or verse stands out to you from this passage? Why?

- Where did Jesus and his family end up? What does Matthew say this fulfilled about Jesus?

- Spend time thinking today about how God knows all the circumstances of our lives, and has a purpose for all of them.

Day 7: Matthew 2

Read through the whole chapter and write out the verse that spoke to you most this week. Meditate on that verse today—and for an extra challenge, memorize it!

3. PREPARING THE WAY
Matthew 3

LEADER'S INSIGHT

Of all the people God could choose to introduce the ministry of Jesus, John the Baptist seems like the least likely candidate. He wore camel hair, ate locusts, and screamed words that were abrasive and offensive. If I were God, I might have made a different choice.

And yet, it is clear that John the Baptist had a personality that drew people, and not just a few of them. The beginning of Matthew 3 says that people came from Jerusalem, Judea, and "the whole region of the Jordan." The only way to explain his appeal was that God anointed him. In Isaiah 40:3, we see that God had John in mind even before he was born.

This chapter reveals that God often chooses the least likely person to accomplish his work. In some ways, it makes his presence even more apparent. Your students will see that even though John the Baptist was not much to look at from the outside, his words reveal his reverence for God. And he never let his ego stand in the way of pointing to Jesus.

Like a best man at a wedding, John knew his role. He didn't try to be the main attraction; instead, he pointed to the main attraction.

In that, he is a model for us all.

Share

- Have you ever heard words of wisdom from someone you didn't expect? If so, when?

- Have you ever been baptized? If so, when? What effect (if any) did it have in your life?

- When you think of the Holy Spirit, what image comes to your mind? In what way do you think the Holy Spirit changes people?

Observe

Observation Questions

- Where did John the Baptist come from, and what was his message? (verses 1-2) What Old Testament prophecy does John fulfill? (verse 3)

- How is John the Baptist described in verse 4? What does he say/do to the people who come to him? (verses 5-6)

- What does John the Baptist say to the Pharisees and Sadducees? (verses 7-10) What does he say about Jesus? (verse 11)

- According to verse 15, why does John baptize Jesus? What happens when Jesus is baptized? (verses 16-17)

Think

Interpretation Questions

- In what way(s) did John the Baptist prepare the way for Jesus? How did he fulfill the prophecy in verse 3?

- Why do you think John spoke so harshly to the Sadducees and Pharisees? What clues do you get about them in verses 7-10?

- What do John's words in verses 11-14 show you about his character? How did he think of himself next to Jesus?

- Do you think anyone saw the dove and heard the words God spoke when Jesus was baptized? What do you imagine the scene looked like to those who were watching?

Apply

Application Questions

- Do you ever repent? If so, when? What do you think repentance means?

- What would you have thought about John the Baptist if you saw him? What does this tell you about the way we judge people?

- How is John a model for us when people see we are doing great things for God? What should our attitude be?

- What does the Holy Spirit's presence look like in your life? Do you feel God's presence inside you? If so, what does it feel like?

Do

Optional Activity

If you were preparing people for the coming of Jesus, how would you do it? Have students write their best ideas anonymously and put them in a pile. Read them out loud (without saying who wrote which one) and vote as a group which idea you think would be most effective. Give a jar of honey to the winner.

QUIET TIME REFLECTIONS

Day 1: Matthew 3:1-3

- What word or verse stands out to you from this passage? Why?

- What prophecy did John the Baptist fulfill? (See Isaiah 40:3.)

- Spend time thinking today about how John's whole purpose was to introduce Jesus to the world.

Day 2: Matthew 3:4-6

- What word or verse stands out to you from this passage? Why?

- What did John do for the people? What do you think people thought of him?

- Spend time thinking today about how you form impressions of people and what you would have thought of John the Baptist.

Day 3: Matthew 3:7-10

- What word or verse stands out to you from this passage? Why?

- What does John know about the Pharisees and Sadducees? Who do you think looked more religious, the Pharisees or John?

- Spend time thinking today about how faith is shown by the fruit of our lives, not our religious activity.

Day 4: Matthew 3:11-12

- What word or phrase stands out to you from these verses? Why?

- How does John compare his baptism to Jesus' baptism?

- Spend time thinking today about the difference between someone who leads you to Christ and the work of Christ himself.

Day 5: Matthew 3:13-15

- What word or phrase stands out to you from these verses? Why?

- What did John say to Jesus when he came to be baptized? Why did he consent to baptize him?

- Spend time thinking today about the way Jesus humbled himself and allowed others to be used in his ministry.

Day 6: Matthew 3:16-17

- What word or phrase stands out to you from these verses? Why?

- How did the voice from heaven confirm who Jesus was?

- Spend time thinking today about the way you "hear" from God.

Day 7: Matthew 3

Read through the whole chapter and write out the verse that spoke to you most this week. Meditate on that verse today—and for an extra challenge, memorize it!

4. TESTED AND TRIED
Matthew 4

LEADER'S INSIGHT

Before Jesus begins his ministry, he is sent to "boot camp" to be prepared for the task. Here in the desert, alone with the devil, a great spiritual battle is won.

With each "no" to what Satan offers, Jesus says "yes" to what God has. By looking at Jesus' confrontation in the desert, we see how temptation can be used by God to strengthen our spiritual muscles—much like exercising can be used to strengthen our physical muscles. Our resistance is bolstered or weakened by our response.

The more we give in, the weaker we become; the more we resist, the stronger we will be. Here in the desert, Jesus laid the foundation for his course; and it strengthened him for his future. This culminated in his greatest battle in the Garden of Gethsemane. Ultimately, he was able to choose God's path, even though it meant his death.

In this chapter, your students will see that Jesus was tempted in every way that we are, yet he did not give in. By saying no to the physical satisfaction, power, and wealth that the devil offered, he said yes to the satisfaction, power, and spiritual wealth that only God can give. For that reason, we don't remember him as "Jesus the Great." We remember him as Jesus our Lord.

Share

- Which of these three are you most tempted by?

    Wealth (acquiring things you want)

    Satisfaction (eating, drinking, physical pleasure)

    Power (status, what people think of you)

- Do you think temptation strengthens us or weakens us? Why?

- Would you consider yourself a follower of Jesus? If so, what compelled you to follow him?

Observe

Observation Questions

- Where was Jesus led to be tempted by the Devil? (verse 1) What condition does verse 2 say he was in?

- What were the three temptations the Devil presented to Jesus? (verses 3, 6, 8-9) What was Jesus' response?

- Where did Jesus go after he was tempted? What prophecy did this fulfill? (verse 14)

- Who were the four disciples Jesus called first to follow him? (verses 18, 21) How long did it take them to decide whether or not to go? (verses 20, 22)

Think

Interpretation Questions

- What does Jesus use to combat the Devil when he is being tempted? What do the three words he repeats each time tell you about each response?

- Why do you think Jesus is tempted just before he begins his ministry? What purpose might God have had in his temptation?

- What does the prophecy in verses 15-16 indicate about Jesus' ministry? Who did he come to reach? Why is he referred to as "a light?"

- Why do you think the disciples dropped everything to follow Jesus? What does this indicate about the way Jesus calls people?

Apply

Application Questions

- Was there a time when you remember being tempted and you resisted? If so, what helped you resist?

- Where (or with whom) are you most likely to give into temptation? Is there a circumstance, place, or person that tends to make you more vulnerable? How can you avoid this?

- Have you said yes to following Jesus? If so, when? If not, what is holding you back?

- Do people in your life know you are a follower of Jesus? What in your life is different because of this decision?

Do

Optional Activity

Have your students choose a discipline over the next week—fasting from a certain food (sweets, snacks, etc.) or media (phones, TV, Facebook), and write down their reflections on their experience. Did they feel stronger or weaker as the week progressed? Why? What purpose might God have for discipline and temptation? Do we discipline ourselves so God will like us more? Or do we do it for some other benefit in our spiritual life?

QUIET TIME REFLECTIONS

Day 1: Matthew 4:1-4

- What word or verse stands out to you from this passage? Why?

- How does Jesus answer the first temptation? How does that speak to you today?

- Spend time thinking today about how our souls are empowered by God's word as much as our bodies are empowered by food.

Day 2: Matthew 4:5-7

- What word or verse stands out to you from this passage? Why?

- How does Jesus answer the second temptation? How does that speak to you today?

- Spend time thinking today about the difference between trusting God and testing him.

Day 3: Matthew 4:8-11

- What word or verse stands out to you from this passage? Why?

- How does Jesus answer the final temptation? How does that speak to you today?

- Spend time thinking today about the ways we worship other things besides God.

Day 4: Matthew 4:12-17

- What word or verse stands out to you from this passage? Why?

- What prophecy did Jesus living in Capernaum fulfill? (See Isaiah 9:12.) How are the prophecies further proof that Jesus was the awaited Messiah?

- Spend time thinking today about how Jesus fulfills the prophecies in the Old Testament, and how that is further proof that he was and is the Messiah.

Day 5: Matthew 4:18-22

- What word or verse stands out to you from this passage? Why?

- How did Peter and Andrew respond to Jesus when he asked them to follow him? Do you respond to Jesus this way?

- Spend time thinking today about how you respond to Jesus when he is leading you. How can you tell when he is calling you to do something?

Day 6: Matthew 4:23-25

- What word or verse stands out to you from this passage? Why?

- What news do you think "spread all over" about Jesus? What do you think people were saying about him?

- Spend time thinking today about how you can spread the word about Jesus. Is there one person you could talk to about him?

Day 7: Matthew 4

Read through the whole chapter and write out the verse that spoke to you most this week. Meditate on that verse today—and for an extra challenge, memorize it!

5. HOW TO TREAT OTHERS
Matthew 5

LEADER'S INSIGHT

Over the next three chapters, we are presented with the only sermon Jesus ever gave. And it's clear from the start that he's advocating a very different way to live. The "blessings" described in the Beatitudes are not blessings we normally hear about; they run counter to the culture we live. However when we live this way, we permeate our culture with the presence of God.

In this chapter, students will have a chance to reflect on their influence, for better or for worse. Jesus makes it clear that it is through our relationships with others that our relationship with God is shown. Perhaps the words of the simple song say it best: "They will know we are Christians by our love." However, it is only through God's strength that we can live this out.

So how do we do that? We're the first to make up when it's not our fault. We keep our commitments even when others haven't. We don't fight back when people deserve it. We love people who hate us. According to Jesus' words, this is how our relationships should look when we want to point people to something greater than ourselves.

Apparently God doesn't want us to just talk about his love. He wants us to live it.

Share

- Do you think the world defines blessing the same way God does? Why/Why not?

- If you had to sum up in one phrase how you treat others, what would it be? Does your faith impact the way you treat others?

- Which is hardest for you to do?

  A. Share your faith with others,

  B. Not take revenge

  C. Not talk about people behind their backs,

  D. Love your enemies.

  Why is it hardest?

Observe

Observation Questions

- What are the eight traits Jesus calls "blessed" in the Beatitudes? (verses 3-10) Why does he say we should rejoice when we are persecuted? (verse 12)

- What does Jesus say we are in verses 13 and 14? What is the result of letting our light shine in verse 16?

- What does Jesus say we are to do before we go to the altar to worship God? (verses 23-24) How does Jesus sum up the way we keep our oaths to people? (verse 37)

- What does Jesus say about payback in verses 38-40? What does he say about how we are to treat our enemies? (verses 43-44) What reason does he give for why he says this in verses 46-47?

Think

Interpretation Questions

- How are the Beatitudes different from what the world calls "blessed"? (Give specific examples from verses 3-11.)

- What does it mean to be "salt" as a Christian? What does it mean to be "light?" How are they different?

- Why do you think Jesus says we should make things right in our relationships before we go to him? (verses 23-24) How do our relationships with others affect our relationship with God?

- What do you think Jesus means in verses 38-42? Is he being literal? Why does he say we should love our enemies? (verses 43-46)

Apply

Application Questions

- Which Beatitude in verses 3-11 do you have the hardest time living out? Which is the easiest for you to live out?

- Are you better at being salt or light as a Christian? Which do you need to work on in your Christian life right now?

- Is there a broken relationship in your life that you need to make right? If so, what steps will you take to make that happen?

- When you read Jesus' commandment to love your enemies, is there someone who comes to mind? Write that person's initials next to that verse and pray for your relationship with them this week.

Do

Optional Activity

Have popcorn or chips in three bowls prepared three ways: Without salt, with salt, and over-salted. After your students taste them, have them choose the one they liked best, and the one they liked least. Debrief the exercise asking what it means to be salt as a Christian, and what it looks like when we are "under-salted" or "over-salted." Added bonus: Give students a saltshaker with the verse.

QUIET TIME REFLECTIONS

Day 1: Matthew 5:1-12

- What word or verse stands out to you from this passage? Why?

- Which Beatitude is the most challenging for you? What makes it challenging?

- Spend time thinking today about how you can live out the Beatitudes in your life.

Day 2: Matthew 5:13-20

- What word or verse stands out to you from this passage? Why?

- What is the difference between being "salt" and being "light"? Which do you have a harder time with?

- Spend time thinking today about how you can be salt and light in the midst of your friends, family, and school.

Day 3: Matthew 5:21-26

- What word or verse stands out to you from this passage? Why?

- In what ways do we "murder" each other with the things we say? Is there anyone you need to go to and ask forgiveness for something you did?

- Spend time thinking today about how to build others up rather than tearing them down.

Day 4: Matthew 5:27-32

- What word or verse stands out to you from this passage? Why?

- What does your reading teach you today about the commitment of marriage? What does it teach you about the way to prepare for marriage sexually and spiritually?

- Say a prayer for your future spouse today, and spend time thinking about how he/she would like you to be preparing for your marriage.

Day 5: Matthew 5:33-42

- What word or verse stands out to you from this passage? Why?

- What does Jesus say about giving people what they deserve? How does our forgiveness and grace show the presence of God in us?

- Spend time thinking today about how you can show grace to someone who doesn't deserve it.

Day 6: Matthew 5:43-47

- What word or verse stands out to you from this passage? Why?

- How does loving an enemy reveal the power of God? Is this possible for you?

- Spend time thinking today about how God's love can fuel you in loving others.

Day 7: Matthew 5

Read through the whole chapter and write out the verse that spoke to you most this week. Meditate on that verse today, and for an extra challenge, memorize it!

6. HOW TO LIVE BY FAITH
Matthew 6

LEADER'S INSIGHT

A pastor once said to me, "What you live is what you believe, and everything else is just talk." He's right. We can talk all we want about Jesus. But our actions reveal our belief.

Frederick Buechner puts it this way: *"You know who you are by where your feet take you."* Certainly Jesus' words in this chapter echo these sentiments. Jesus contrasts what it means to do your acts of righteousness for the audience around you with what it means to do your acts of righteousness for an audience of one. The ability to do the latter reveals the presence of faith.

Here in this chapter your students will wrestle with the righteousness Jesus describes. Living this way is challenging. We have an innate desire for others to notice the good that we do. Think about it: When was the last time you did something admirable and didn't tell anyone about it?

Someone once gave me a piece of wisdom that is a good way to sum up Jesus' words in the Sermon on the Mount. "Show when you are tempted to hide, and hide when you are tempted to show."

If we all did that, the world might think differently about Christians.

Share

- Is prayer something you do every day, every once in a while, or only when you need something? What do you think prayer accomplishes?

- When it comes to money, would you say your treasure is on earth or in heaven? Why?

- On a scale of 1-10 (1= hardly at all, 10 = a lot), how much do you worry? What do you worry about most?

Observe

Observation Questions

- What does Jesus say will happen if you do your "acts of righteousness" to be seen by others? (verse 1) What will happen if you do them secretly? (verse 4)

- When we pray, what does Jesus say we have to do to receive God's forgiveness? (verses 14-15)

- What does Jesus say is the difference between treasure on earth and treasure in heaven? (verses 19-20)

- What two examples does Jesus give when he tells us not to worry? (verses 26, 28)

Think

Interpretation Questions

- Why do you think Jesus wants us to do our acts of righteousness in secret?

- What does the Lord's Prayer teach us about how to pray? (verses 9-13) How should we start our prayers? What should we pray for?

- What do you think it means to store up treasure in heaven? What are some examples of doing that?

- Why does Jesus tell us not to worry? What does it do to our faith?

Apply

Application Questions

- Do you struggle with doing good things so others can see? Why/why not? How hard is it for you to do good things anonymously?

- If the Lord's Prayer can be summed up with the acronym "ACTS" (Adoration, Confession, Thanksgiving, Supplication), which of these four do you need to work on most?

- Do you think fasting is always about food? What are some other ways we can fast? What would be hardest for you to give up?

- What is your biggest worry right now? Commit to praying about it every time it comes to your mind. Choose a prayer partner in your small group who can help you with this.

Do

Optional Activity

Have the students in your group think of "acts of righteousness" they could do this week, and write them on a piece of paper (without their names). You collect them; when your group comes back, have your group members raise their hands if they were able to do their act of righteousness. Count the hands and then read the papers, thanking God for the acts that were done (without knowing which ones). This is a chance for your group to celebrate what they did, without giving credit to any one person. (It's also a sneaky way to make your kids want to live their faith!)

QUIET TIME REFLECTIONS

Day 1: Matthew 6:1-4

- What word or verse stands out to you from this passage? Why?

- What does Jesus say about our giving? How can you practice this today?

- Spend time thinking today about the different things you can give, and how you can give them the way Jesus says.

Day 2: Matthew 6:5-8

- What word or verse stands out to you from this passage? Why?

- How does Jesus say we should pray? How shouldn't we pray?

- Spend time thinking today about your prayer life and how Jesus' words can lead you in it.

Day 3: Matthew 6:9-15

- What word or verse stands out to you from this passage? Why?

- When did you learn the Lord's Prayer? What do these words mean to you when you pray?

- Spend time today praying the Lord's Prayer sentence by sentence so you can think about what you are saying.

Day 4: Matthew 6:16-18

- What word or verse stands out to you from this passage? Why?

- Have you ever fasted? What meal can you skip today so you can focus more on God?

- Spend time praying today during your mini fast, and practice doing it the way Jesus describes in this passage.

Day 5: Matthew 6:19-24

- What word or verse stands out to you from this passage? Why?

- Where does Jesus say our treasure should be? Is that where yours is?

- Spend time thinking today about your treasure, and how you can invest in things that will last.

Day 6: Matthew 6:25-34

- What word or verse stands out to you from this passage? Why?

- Do you struggle with worry? What things are you concerned about today? How does this passage speak to those concerns?

- Spend time today praying for the things you are worrying about. Every time you are tempted to worry, pray instead!

Day 7: Matthew 6

Read through the whole chapter and write out the verse that spoke to you most this week. Meditate on that verse today—and for an extra challenge, memorize it!

7. TRUE JUDGMENT
Matthew 7

LEADER'S INSIGHT

I was sitting with my students at a youth camp when the speaker came out with his back to the audience. There was a wide headband around the back of his head. As he spoke, he turned around, and he revealed that the headband was attached to a giant rubber log sticking out of his eye. The visual was so stark (not to mention hilarious) that it was all I remembered from that evening's talk. And given that his theme was "judging others," it was a brilliant teaching tool.

He borrowed the idea from Jesus.

One thing your students will observe about Jesus is that he is a master teacher. He was the guy you'd want to invite as your camp speaker. He told stories and painted pictures that penetrated people's hearts. And even if they didn't accept what he said, they remembered it. This was evident in the Pharisees' response.

At the end of this chapter, Matthew says, *"The crowds were amazed at his teaching because he taught as one who had authority, and not as their teachers of the law."* They could see the difference between teaching that comes from what you know, and teaching that comes from who you are.

Jesus didn't just teach his lessons. He lived them.

Share

- Do you think others would describe you as judgmental or nonjudgmental? Why?

- Do you believe God gives us everything we pray for? Why/Why not?

- Would you say the way you live is a good reflection of what you believe? If so, how? If not, why not?

Observe

Observation Questions

- How does Jesus say we will be judged? (verse 2) What are we to do before we judge others? (verse 5)

- What analogy does Jesus use in verses 9-11 to describe the way God answers our prayers? What does he say in verse 12 about the way we are to treat others?

- According to Jesus, can a bad tree bear good fruit? (verse 18) How do we recognize whether a tree is good or bad? (verse 20)

- When a storm comes, which house stands firm according to Jesus? (verse 25) Which house falls? (verse 26) What kind of house does a wise man build? (verse 24)

Think

Interpretation Questions

- What do you think Jesus means when he says to remove the plank from our eye before we remove a speck from someone else's?

- Do you think verses 7-8 means that we get everything we pray for? Why/why not? How does Jesus' analogy in verses 9-11 explain the way God answers prayer?

- How does Jesus describe false prophets in verse 15? Can you think of any examples of the false prophets Jesus describes? Why do you think it is important to avoid them?

- Why do you think it is important to do the words Jesus says? How are his words different than other words you read?

Apply

Application Questions

- If you had to name one foundation upon which you're building your life, what would it be? What in your life right now shows that this is true?

- Do you think Jesus would say you are a tree that produces good fruit, bad fruit, or no fruit? Why? What would you need to do to produce more good fruit?

- Can you think of a time when you've judged someone for a speck in his or her eye when you've had a log in your own eye?

- How many of Jesus' words would you say you act on? 100 percent? 75 percent? 50 percent? 25 percent? What (if anything) keeps you from acting on all his words?

Do

Optional Activity

Take one passage from this chapter and conduct a "Bible doing" rather than a Bible reading. Decide as a group how you will actually live out something Jesus is telling us to do. (This is a great idea for all Bible studies!)

QUIET TIME REFLECTIONS

Day 1: Matthew 7:1-6

- What word or verse stands out to you from this passage? Why?

- Do you tend to be judgmental of others? How does this passage speak to you today?

- Spend time thinking today about whether you have a plank in your own eye while you are focused on the speck in someone else's eye. How does this help you be less judgmental of others?

Day 2: Matthew 7:7-12

- What word or verse stands out to you from this passage? Why?

- How does Jesus compare God's gifts to our parents' gifts? What does this reveal to you about the way God loves you?

- Spend time thinking today about how much God loves you, and that he answers your prayers according to what is best for you.

Day 3: Matthew 7:13-14

- What word or phrase stands out to you from these verses? Why?

- Why do you think Jesus says the road that leads to life is narrow? Are you on it?

- Spend time thinking today about how Jesus is the only road that can lead us to God.

Day 4: Matthew 7:15-20

- What word or verse stands out to you from this passage? Why?

- How are we supposed to recognize false prophets? Have you ever experienced this? How will you protect yourself from this?

- Spend time thinking today about the importance of looking inward to judge someone, and how the more you know God's word, the less you will be deceived.

Day 5: Matthew 7:21-23

- What word or phrase stands out to you from these verses? Why?

- What does Jesus say about the people who will enter the kingdom of heaven? What do you think it means to do God's will?

- Spend time thinking today about whether you are doing God's will. You can start anytime!

Day 6: Matthew 7:24-29

- What word or verse stands out to you from this passage? Why?

- What kind of house do you want to build? According to Jesus, what do you need to do to build it?

- Spend time thinking today about whether you are living out your faith in your actions. It's never too late to begin.

Day 7: Matthew 7

Read through the whole chapter and write out the verse that spoke to you most this week. Meditate on that verse today—and for an extra challenge, memorize it!

8. FAITH AND HEALING
Matthew 8

LEADER'S INSIGHT

If you've been a Christian long enough, you may have seen God heal. And you probably have seen him NOT heal—at least in the way that you were asking. What then?

One response is to let it weaken your faith. *If God doesn't do what I am asking, why should I believe in him?* But God isn't a genie in a bottle; he is a living active Creator who sees beyond what we can see. His ways are not our ways. And our lives are bigger than this life. As spectacular as healings can be, they do not change the fact that one day every one of us will die. For that reason, we need more than a healer. We need a Savior.

So how are our prayers for healing connected to our faith? Like all of our prayers, Jesus makes it clear that our faith does make a difference. However, faith is best exercised when we still believe, even when the answer is different than what we pray for. Believing God *can* do it is different than believing God *will* do it. The former makes God's will, rather than ours, the center of our prayers.

In this chapter, your students will see that while God cares for our physical well-being, what he cares most about is our eternal well-being. So his healing us takes shape in many ways. Because of that, we can say with confidence that God does heal and trust that in his healing, it's our spiritual health that he cares about most.

Share

- On a scale of 1-10 , how much faith do you have? (1=hardly any, 10=a lot)

- Have you ever prayed for healing and had it happen? Have you ever prayed for healing and had it not happen?

- What is the greatest miracle you have ever witnessed?

Observe

Observation Questions

- What does Jesus say to the man with leprosy after he heals him? (verse 3) What does he tell him to do?

- How does the centurion respond to Jesus when he tells him he will heal his servant? (verses 8-9) What does Jesus say about the centurion? (verse 10)

- What does Jesus say to the teacher of the law who wants to follow him? (verse 20) What does he say to the man who wants to bury his father before he follows him? (verse 22)

- What does Jesus say to his disciples when they are afraid of the storm? (verse 26) What does he do next?

Think

Interpretation Questions

- Why do you think Jesus tells the man he healed of leprosy not to tell anyone? Do you think he was keeping his identity a secret for a reason?

- Why was Jesus so impressed with the centurion's faith? (verse 10) Do you think this relates to what Jesus says in verses 11-12? If so, how?

- Do Jesus' comments in verses 20 and 22 seem harsh to you? Why do you think he responds that way to the two who want to follow him?

- What do the two accounts in verses 23-34 communicate about the extent of Jesus' power? Do you think these events help prove he was the Son of God?

Apply

Application Questions

- If you could ask Jesus to do anything for you, what would it be?

- Is there someone in your life you admire for his or her faith? If so, whom?

- Has there ever been a storm in your life that caused you to feel afraid? Have you ever experienced God's peace in a storm?

- Have you ever seen or experienced God's healing in yourself or someone you know? Have you ever experienced God not healing when you wanted him to? What do you think is the purpose of God's healing?

Do

Optional Activity

Invite an architect or builder to your group and have him/her share the importance of a foundation when building a house. (Encourage pictures.) If you can't find anyone, do a search on the Internet and find some pictures of houses that stood or fell apart because of their foundation.

QUIET TIME REFLECTIONS

Day 1: Matthew 8:1-3

- What word or verse stands out to you from this passage? Why?

- How does the man with leprosy ask Jesus for healing? What does that tell you about the way we should pray?

- Spend time thinking today about how to begin or end your prayers with the phrase "If you are willing."

Day 2: Matthew 8:4-13

- What word or verse stands out to you from this passage? Why?

- Why is Jesus astonished at the centurion's faith? Do you trust Jesus this way?

- Spend time thinking today about the areas of your life where you need to trust Jesus more.

Day 3: Matthew 8:14-17

- What word or verse stands out to you from this passage? Why?

- How does Jesus fulfill prophecy in this passage? What does Isaiah 53:4 say about him?

- Spend time thinking today about Jesus as our healer. What do you need healing from today?

Day 4: Matthew 8:18-22

- What word or verse stands out to you from this passage? Why?

- What are some of the hard things Jesus says about following him in this passage? What would you have a hard time leaving behind to follow him?

- Spend time thinking today about how following Jesus costs you. What do you need to give up?

Day 5: Matthew 8:23-27

- What word or verse stands out to you from this passage? Why?

- What is Jesus doing in the middle of the storm? What does that tell you about the storms in your life?

- Spend time thinking today about how you can experience Jesus' peace in the midst of your storms.

Day 6: Matthew 8:28-34

- What word or verse stands out to you from this passage? Why?

- What do the demons call Jesus? What does that tell you about his authority?

- Spend time thinking today about Jesus' power—not just over this world, but the eternal world beyond our sight.

Day 7: Matthew 8

Read through the whole chapter and write out the verse that spoke to you most this week. Meditate on that verse today—and for an extra challenge, memorize it!

9. A DEEPER HEALING
Matthew 9

LEADER'S INSIGHT

I can remember the first time I watched one of those Christian healing TV shows, and saw a person in a wheelchair get up and walk—apparently for the first time. Though I was skeptical about what was happening, the audience was eating it up.

Looking at this chapter made me wonder what would have happened if the healer said to the man in the wheelchair, "Your sins are forgiven." What a letdown that would have been! Yet according to Jesus, that healing makes the greatest difference in someone's life.

Throughout this book, your students will see that Jesus is more concerned with our eternal selves than our physical selves, though there are times when he heals them both. However, the way he heals reveals his heart. Before the healings occur in this chapter, a paralytic is forgiven, a socially outcast woman is prioritized, and an official's daughter is made to wait. Jesus bestowed forgiveness, favor, and humility, and these things took priority before the outside healings were performed.

If we look closely at the healings of Jesus, the way he did them reveals more than the healings themselves. This is the mystery and the greatness of our God.

Share

- Which do you think God values most: healing or forgiveness? Why?

- Have you ever been with the "wrong crowd"? If so, did they influence you, or did you influence them?

- Which miracle would you like to see most: A paralyzed man walking, a blind person seeing, or someone dead brought back to life? Why?

Observe

Observation Questions

- What does Jesus say first when a paralytic is brought to him for healing? (verse 2) What reason does Jesus give in verse 6 for healing him?

- Why does Jesus say he eats with tax collectors and sinners? (verse 12) Who does he say he has come to call? (verse 13)

- Who was Jesus going to heal in verses 18-19? What did he do along the way? (verses 20-22) What happened when he arrived at the ruler's house? (verse 23)

- What does Jesus ask the blind men after they cried out for healing? (verse 28) What does he say while he is healing them? (verse 29) Do they listen to his request not to tell anyone? (verse 31)

Think

Interpretation Questions

- Why do you think Jesus forgave the paralytic's sins before healing him? (verses 2-7)

- What do you think Jesus means in verse 13 when he says, "I desire mercy, not sacrifice"?

- Why do you think Jesus gives the analogy about wineskins when he is talking to the Pharisees in verses 14-17? Do you think it relates at all to verse 13?

- How does Jesus show the importance of faith in verses 27-34? What do the Pharisees' words in verse 34 tell you about their relationship with Jesus?

Apply
Application Questions

- Have you ever made an effort to bring a friend to Jesus? If so, when? If not, why not?

- Is there a friend (or group of friends) who would be hard to picture following Jesus? How do verses 9-13 encourage you to pray for him or her?

- Do you ever get frustrated waiting for Jesus to answer your prayers? Have you ever looked back and seen the reason he was waiting?

- Is it hard for you to have faith that God can do anything? Why/why not? What is hardest for you to believe?

Do
Optional Activity

Make a list of all the people who experienced healing in this chapter (the paralytic, Matthew, the ruler and his daughter, the bleeding woman, the two blind men, the mute man). Have the students share what they think the "deeper healing" was for each one. How was it different from the physical healing they experienced? (Answers: paralytic: sins forgiven; Matthew: social inclusion; the ruler/his daughter: he had to wait until his daughter died and then he had to trust Jesus; the bleeding woman: received attention where she was normally an outcast; the two blind men: had to exercise belief first; the mute man: freed from the demon.)

QUIET TIME REFLECTIONS

Day 1: Matthew 9:1-8

- What word or verse stands out to you from this passage? Why?

- What did the men who brought the paralytic want for him? What did Jesus give him?

- Spend time thinking today about the difference between being healed spiritually and physically.

Day 2: Matthew 9:9-13

- What word or verse stands out to you from this passage? Why?

- How does Matthew experience healing in this passage? Was it physical or social healing?

- Spend time thinking today about how Jesus includes those who would normally be socially outcast—we are all equal in God's kingdom. Who can you include today?

Day 3: Matthew 9:14-17

- What word or verse stands out to you from this passage? Why?

- What does Jesus say about the disciples fasting while he's there? When are the best times to fast?

- Spend time thinking today about someone or something you could fast for today. Give something up as you pray for them and focus on what they need.

Day 4: Matthew 9:18-26

- What word or verse stands out to you from this passage? Why?

- What two people were healed in this passage? In what order were they healed? How did Jesus do for both of them more than they asked?

- Spend time thinking today about how Jesus might be working in your circumstances to heal something in you.

Day 5: Matthew 9:27-34

- What word or verse stands out to you from this passage? Why?

- What does Jesus say when he heals the two blind men? What does that tell you about the importance of our faith in healing?

- Spend time thinking today about your faith and where you need more of it.

Day 6: Matthew 9:35-37

- What word or verse stands out to you from this passage? Why?

- How does Jesus feel about the crowds around him? Do you feel that way about people who don't know Jesus?

- Spend time thinking today about your compassion for others who don't know Jesus. Who needs you to share with them the good news?

Day 7: Matthew 9

Read through the whole chapter and write out the verse that spoke to you most this week. Meditate on that verse today—and for an extra challenge, memorize it!

10. A CALL TO FOLLOWERS
Matthew 10

LEADER'S INSIGHT

In this chapter, Jesus reminds me of a coach. He huddles up the disciples to give them directions for what they're about to do. As followers we have the privilege of representing Jesus as we do his work. And he warns the disciples (and us) of the persecution we may have to endure while they (and we) are doing it.

However, unlike a coach, Jesus is able to promise his disciples that they will have a power greater than themselves inside them, helping them. Coaches merely send their players out, relying on their own strength and talents. Jesus sends us out relying on his strength in our talents. Thankfully there is a big difference.

Your students will discover in this chapter that Jesus calls his followers to spread his word. However, we are not responsible for how people respond. The mystery of spiritual responsiveness is that we cannot control or predict it. Some we think will respond will not. Others we think will never respond will. We invite; God calls. And because we never know when God is knocking on the door of someone's heart, we proceed in courage and live in hope.

This chapter makes it clear that following Jesus and sharing our faith is not easy. However there is nothing greater than being the messenger of faith when people respond.

Share

- Have you ever had a coach or teacher who inspired you and made a difference in the way you live? Can you remember anything he/she said?

- What do you think is the greatest challenge about being a follower of Christ?

- Is it hard or easy for you to share your faith with others? Why?

Observe

Observation Questions

- What did Jesus give his disciples authority to do? (verse 1) What were the names of the disciples? (verses 2-4) Which ones were brothers?

- Where did Jesus send his disciples? (verse 6) What did he tell them to pack? (verse 9)

- What does Jesus say might happen to the disciples in verses 17-18? Why aren't they supposed to worry about what to say? (verses 19-20)

- Why does Jesus tell the disciples not to be afraid of what might happen to them? (verses 26-31) What does he say about the way God loves them?

Think

Interpretation Questions

- What do you think Jesus means in verse 13? How are we supposed to respond to people who reject us?

- What do you think Jesus means when he tells his disciples to be as shrewd as snakes and as innocent as doves? (verse 16) How is this possible?

- What does Jesus mean when he tells the disciples that the Holy Spirit will speak through them? (verse 20) How can we tell when this is happening?

- Since Jesus is referred to as the prince of peace, what do you think he means in verses 34-35? What kind of peace is he talking about here?

Apply

Application Questions

- Have you ever gone door to door to share your faith? Is that something you would ever do? Why/Why not?

- What do you think is the most effective way to share your faith with someone? When was the last time you did it? What keeps you from it, if anything?

- Have you ever had the experience of the Holy Spirit guiding your words or actions? If so, when? If not, would you be responsive if you ever felt prompted by God to do/say something?

- Is there someone in your life right now with whom you could share your faith? If so, what is one action step you could take this week toward doing that?

Do

Optional Activity

Have everyone in the group put down a name on a sheet of paper of someone they would like to become a believer. Put the names in a box or hat, and have everyone draw one. Give the assignment of having each person in your group pray for his/her name over the coming year.

QUIET TIME REFLECTIONS

Day 1: Matthew 10:1-4

- What word or verse stands out to you from this passage? Why?

- What are the names of the 12 disciples? Were there any on the list you didn't know?

- Spend time thinking today about the variety of people Jesus calls to follow him. Is there anyone you need to pray for that he/she would decide to follow Christ?

Day 2: Matthew 10:5-10

- What word or verse stands out to you from this passage? Why?

- What does Jesus tell his disciples in this passage? What authority does he give them to do?

- Spend time thinking today about the authority we have as Christ's followers to do his work. Where are you doing Jesus' work?

Day 3: Matthew 10:11-20

- What word or verse stands out to you from this passage? Why?

- What warnings does Jesus give the disciples in this passage? What does Jesus say will happen to them when they are speaking (in verse 20)? Have you experienced this?

- Spend time thinking today about how the Holy Spirit helps you to say the right thing when you are doing Jesus' work. Where can you make yourself available to do that?

Day 4: Matthew 10:21-31

- What word or verse stands out to you from this passage? Why?

- What does Jesus say will happen because we are his followers? What does he say in verse 26 about the end result?

- Spend time thinking today about how we are sometimes called to suffer as Christians, but in the end, all will be made right.

Day 5: Matthew 10:32-38

- What word or verse stands out to you from this passage? Why?

- What do you think Jesus means when he says we have to love him more than anyone—even family? Is that true for you?

- Spend time thinking today about the priority God has in your life.

Day 6: Matthew 10:39-42

- What word or verse stands out to you from this passage? Why?

- How does verse 39 explain what it means to be a Christian? According to the verses that follow, how close are we to Jesus when we share his message?

- Spend time thinking today about whether or not you have lost your life for Jesus' sake. What would that mean for you?

Day 7: Matthew 10

Read through the whole chapter and write out the verse that spoke to you most this week. Meditate on that verse today, and for an extra challenge, memorize it!

11. TRUE TO THE END
Matthew 11

LEADER'S INSIGHT

Most of us are good starters. But what really matters is whether or not we're good finishers. That's especially true in the journey of faith.

John the Baptist shows us in this chapter how difficult it can be to persevere in faith when life gets tough. After John spent months pointing others to Jesus, and even baptizing him, in this chapter, we find him in jail questioning Jesus about who he really is. I for one can totally identify with him.

The great news of this chapter is that even though John questions Jesus in his hour of weakness, Jesus still commends him as a great prophet. From this, we see that Jesus understands when our circumstances throw us off in our belief. Your students will observe in this chapter that God is bigger than our questions. And he is okay when we wrestle honestly with them as we pursue our journey of faith.

Ultimately, following Christ is a journey of letting go and trusting him with the circumstances of our lives. In so doing, we discover that his plan often involves something greater than we can perceive. However, we can rest in the trust and knowledge that someone who is bigger than us is orchestrating our lives. And his eyes see ahead to the eternal future we will one day be able to see.

Share

- Have you ever been disillusioned with God? If so, how?

- Who is the godliest person you know? What makes him/her godly?

- Would you describe your soul as weary and burdened or restful and peaceful? Why?

Observe

Observation Questions

- What does John tell his disciples to ask Jesus? (verse 3) How does Jesus respond? (verse 4)

- What does Jesus say about John the Baptist in verses 10-14?

- According to verses 18-19, what did people say about John? What did they say about Jesus (the Son of Man)? According to Jesus' words in verse 19, how is wisdom shown?

- According to verse 27, who knows the Son? Who knows the Father? What does Jesus promise to those who come to him? (verse 28)

Think

Interpretation Questions

- Why do you think John sent his disciples to see if Jesus really was the expected Messiah? (verse 3) Do you think he was discouraged because of his circumstances? How might verse 4 have encouraged him?

- What do you observe about Jesus' relationship to John the Baptist in verses 7-14? What do you think Jesus means by what he says in verse 12?

- How does Jesus show the importance of repentance in verses 20-24? Why should Jesus' miracles lead to repentance? Do you think there is a tie between belief and repentance?

- What do you think Jesus means when he says his yoke is easy and his burden is light? (verse 30)

Apply

Application Questions

- Do you think God's affection for us is shown by our circumstances? How does John's situation in verse 2 help you answer this question?

- When is it hardest for you to be faithful to God? Are there any circumstances or temptations that make it especially tough?

- Do you show your godliness more on the outside (what people see) or on the inside (what God sees)? Which is more important to God?

- Is there a burden you are carrying that Jesus can carry to make your load lighter? If so, what?

Do

Optional Activity

Have your students make a list of the adversities they've faced so far that have made it hard for them to persevere in their faith. Then have them make a list of the things that *would be* really difficult for them to experience and still persevere in their faith. Then ask these questions: How does this story of John the Baptist in jail guide us as we face tough times? What does it tell us about questioning God? How do Jesus' words about John assure us in our doubts? What do you think is really important to God as we persevere in our faith?

QUIET TIME REFLECTIONS

Day 1: Matthew 11:1-6

- What word or verse stands out to you from this passage? Why?

- Why do you think John questioned Jesus when he was in jail? Have you ever questioned whether God really existed or cared?

- Spend time thinking today about how sometimes it doesn't look like God cares, but we will one day see that he always does.

Day 2: Matthew 11:7-15

- What word or verse stands out to you from this passage? Why?

- What does Jesus say about John the Baptist? How does that comfort you based on what John just did?

- Spend time thinking today about how God knows us inside and out, and doesn't judge us when we question him. He wants an honest relationship with us!

Day 3: Matthew 11:16-19

- What word or verse stands out to you from this passage? Why?

- How does Jesus point out in this passage that people only see from the surface? How does the last sentence guide us in the way we should perceive others?

- Spend time thinking today about the phrase "wisdom is proved right by her actions." What does that mean for you?

Day 4: Matthew 11:20-24

- What word or verse stands out to you from this passage? Why?

- How does Jesus show us the importance of repentance in this passage? When was the last time you repented?

- Spend time giving your sins to God, and asking forgiveness for them today.

Day 5: Matthew 11:25-27

- What word or verse stands out to you from this passage? Why?

- What does Jesus say about the way God reveals things to us? Why do you think God reveals more things to children than to the wise?

- Spend time thinking today about how you can be like a child in your faith.

Day 6: Matthew 11:28-30

- What word or verse stands out to you from this passage? Why?

- What does Jesus say we should do when we are burdened? Is there a burden you can bring him today?

Day 7: Matthew 11

Read through the whole chapter and write out the verse that spoke to you most this week. Meditate on that verse today—and for an extra challenge, memorize it!

12. FRUIT SHOWS THE TRUTH
Matthew 12

LEADER'S INSIGHT

Would you recognize an apple tree if you saw it? I wouldn't. Unless, of course, an apple was hanging from one of its branches. With only a glimpse of the tree, I could easily confuse one fruit tree for another. But if I watched that tree long enough, I'd be able to see what kind of tree it was.

This analogy is used by Jesus to describe spiritual judgment. We cannot see from the outside how spiritual a person is. The people who "look" spiritual may actually be the least spiritual; we learn that by watching the Pharisees. They followed the laws perfectly, but missed the point of the laws altogether. And they couldn't let go of their pride long enough to see that the one who *made* the laws was standing in front of them.

What comes out of the Pharisees when Jesus is in their midst betrays the blackness of their hearts. They accuse him of belonging to the Devil and plot together that he must die.

The Pharisees were the closest to God in appearance. But they were farthest from God in their hearts. In this chapter, Jesus shows which matters most.

Share

- Do you think a person's belief is revealed by what one says or how one behaves? Why?

- How would you define God's family? If someone asked you if you were in God's family, how would you answer?

- What do you think is the greatest sign pointing to Jesus being the Son of God? Why?

Observe

Observation Questions

- What was the Pharisees' complaint in verse 2 when they saw what Jesus was doing in verse 1? What does Jesus say about himself in verse 8?

- What did the Pharisees say about Jesus' healing in verse 24? How does Jesus respond to them in verses 25-26?

- What sign does Jesus give for what he will do in verse 40? Who does he compare himself to?

- How does Jesus respond to the question about his family in verse 47? Who does Jesus say are his mother and brothers? (verse 50)

Think

Interpretation Questions

- What do you think Jesus' words in verse 7 mean?

- Why do you think the Pharisees were upset with Jesus when he was healing people? (See verse 14.) What effect did their threats have on Jesus (if any)?

- How do you interpret Jesus' argument in verses 25-28? How do you think his words impacted the Pharisees?

- Do you think Jesus' mother and brothers felt hurt about what Jesus said in verse 48? Or do you think they understood? Why?

Apply

Application Questions

- Do you do (or not do) anything special on the Sabbath? Why/Why not?

- If you were alive when Jesus came, do you think you might have wondered whether Jesus was really the Son of God? Why/Why not? If you are a believer, what convinced you?

- How do people see evidence of your faith in God in your life? What do you do or not do because of your faith?

- On a scale of 1-10, how do you think Jesus would judge you on the basis of your "fruit"? What is one thing you could do to begin producing more fruit?

Do

Optional Activity

Get three different apples: one that isn't ripe yet, one that's just right, and one that's overripe (brown, spotty). Tell your students to choose which apple best represents the fruit of their spiritual life right now—and why.

QUIET TIME REFLECTIONS

Day 1: Matthew 12:1-14

- What word or verse stands out to you from this passage? Why?

- What does Jesus say about the rule the Pharisees had about the Sabbath? What does he do in verse 13? How does this show you what's important and not important with our faith?

- Spend time thinking today about how God wants a relationship with us—not just for us to follow rules.

Day 2: Matthew 12:15-21

- What word or verse stands out to you from this passage? Why?

- What prophecy does Jesus fulfill by healing people and not drawing attention to himself, saying who he was? (See Isaiah 42:1-4.) Why do you think Jesus is quiet about his identity?

- Spend time thinking today about the importance of our faith, and how God leaves room for it.

Day 3: Matthew 12:22-32

- What word or verse stands out to you from this passage? Why?

- How does Jesus answer the accusation that his healing is from the Devil? Why is that impossible according to Jesus?

- Spend time thinking today about the importance of staying connected to God through the Holy Spirit. Observe today what the Holy Spirit feels like inside you.

Day 4: Matthew 12:33-37

- What word or verse stands out to you from this passage? Why?

- What does Jesus say in verse 34 about how our mouths speak? What controls the words we say?

- Spend time thinking today about the way you speak to others, and whether your speech reflects the presence of God.

Day 5: Matthew 12:38-45

- What word or verse stands out to you from this passage? Why?

- Why does Jesus compare himself to Jonah? What are the parallels? How does this foreshadow what is going to happen?

- Spend time thinking today about how Jesus gives us clues about his crucifixion and resurrection throughout his ministry.

Day 6: Matthew 12:46-50

- What word or verse stands out to you from this passage? Why?

- What does Jesus say about his family in this passage? In what way are we like family with other believers?

- Spend time thinking today about the difference between your earthly family and your heavenly family.

Day 7: Matthew 12

Read through the whole chapter and write out the verse that spoke to you most this week. Meditate on that verse today—and for an extra challenge, memorize it!

13. SEEDS AND WEEDS
Matthew 13

LEADER'S INSIGHT

Have you ever grown a plant or tended a garden? If so, you know that most of the action is underneath the soil. What goes on there will determine the life and health of the plant. Even though you can't really see what's happening under the soil, what you do see is how weak or strong the plant becomes. And it's all a result of what's happening under the surface. This "under the surface" work makes soils and seeds one of Jesus' favorite images for describing the spiritual life.

In this chapter, Jesus tells the Parable of the Sower to invite his listeners to choose which kind of soil best describes their spiritual life. He then builds on this analogy with a story about weeds growing alongside seeds, and how they aren't separated until harvest time. Through these images, Jesus paints a vivid picture of our spiritual journey.

The soil we are planted in is important for our growth, but so is adversity. The "weeds" (or difficult people/circumstances) can strengthen or weaken our spiritual growth, depending on our response. We become stronger when we are able to grow in spite of the weeds. This is part of God's strategy, because as we learn in this chapter, they will be with us until the end of our lives.

Through each parable in this chapter, Jesus invites us to see where we are—and what needs to change—to prioritize his kingdom. This will determine how we will be received when we enter in.

Share

- Have you ever planted anything and watched it grow? What do you think is most important for something to grow? What deters growth?

- Have you ever had someone teach you something by telling you a story? If so, did it help you remember the lesson? Why/why not?

- What is the greatest treasure you have? What makes it valuable?

Observe

Observation Questions

- In the Parable of the Sower (verses 1-9), what were the four places that the farmer's seed landed? (verses 4-5, 7-8) What happened to the seeds in each place?

- In the Parable of the Weeds (verses 24-30), what does the owner say about pulling up the weeds? When does he say he will deal with them? (verse 30)

- Jesus compares the kingdom of heaven to five things. What are they? (verses 31, 33, 44, 45, 47)

- Where does Jesus say is the only place a prophet is without honor? (verse 57) What happened in verses 54-56 to make him say this?

Think

Interpretation Questions

- Why do you think Jesus tells the Parable of the Sower? Whom do you think the sower symbolizes? What is the main point of this parable?

- Why do you think Jesus compares the kingdom of heaven to a mustard seed and yeast? How do these things help you understand the kingdom?

- What do the Parables of the Hidden Treasure and the Pearl have in common? Why do you think Jesus makes this point twice?

- How does Jesus relate miracles to faith in verse 58? How do you think the two are tied together?

Apply

Application Questions

- Which of the four soils Jesus describes best represents you? Why?

- What changes do you need to make to be "good soil"? (verse 23)

- When you read the Parable of the Weeds (verses 24-30), what do you think Jesus is saying? How do you apply it to your life?

- How do you understand the kingdom of God? How would you explain it to someone else?

Do

Optional Activity

Buy packets of seeds (the same kind) for each student in your group. Have them plant their seeds at home and record everything they are doing (including where they plant them). When you meet in your group, have a "seed report" where students share how their seeds are doing. This will help your students realize how long it takes for seeds to grow, and what kind of care is conducive to the plant's growth. This activity will provide several analogies for your group throughout your study of Matthew.

QUIET TIME REFLECTIONS

Day 1: Matthew 13:1-23

- What word or verse stands out to you from this passage? Why?

- Which soil best represents where you are today? Where would you like to be?

- Spend time thinking today about the soil that best represents where you are, and what changes (if any) you want to make to be where you want to be.

Day 2: Matthew 13:24-30

- What word or verse stands out to you from this passage? Why?

- What/Who do you think the wheat represents in Jesus' parable?

- Spend time thinking today about Jesus' analogy and how it speaks to your life right now.

Day 3: Matthew 13:31-35

- What word or verse stands out to you from this passage? Why?

- How are the mustard seed and yeast similar in their effect? Why do you think Jesus used these word pictures to describe the kingdom of God?

- Spend time thinking today about how God takes something little and uses it to do something big.

Day 4: Matthew 13:36-43

- What word or verse stands out to you from this passage? Why?

- Why do you think Jesus told the Parable of the Weeds? How does the explanation help you understand it?

- Spend time thinking today about the weeds around you, and what you need to do to not let them affect your growth.

Day 5: Matthew 13:44-46

- What word or verse stands out to you from this passage? Why?

- How do the treasure and the pearl help you understand something else about God's kingdom? What is Jesus trying to say about the kingdom by telling these two short parables?

- Spend time thinking today about what you value, and whether your life reflects that you value the kingdom of God.

Day 6: Matthew 13:47-58

- What word or verse stands out to you from this passage? Why?

- How is the Parable of the Net similar to the Parable of the Weeds? How is it different?

- Spend time thinking today about all the ways Jesus explained the kingdom, and what you've learned about it.

Day 7: Matthew 13

Read through the whole chapter and write out the verse that spoke to you most this week. Meditate on that verse today—and for an extra challenge, memorize it!

14. MIRACLE MAN
Matthew 14

LEADER'S INSIGHT

Have you ever seen a miracle that expanded your view of God? That's what happens to the disciples in this chapter. They had seen Jesus heal, but they hadn't witnessed his eminence over creation. As they watch him make food appear and see him walk on water, they realize in a new way how powerful he is.

In this chapter, your students will be invited to take a look at their image of God, and how much they can really trust him. However, this usually requires us to take a step of faith. In the story of the feeding of the 5,000, they will see that when we give God what little we have, he can multiply it beyond what we imagine.

Then through Peter's story of walking on water, your students will examine where they need to "get out of the boat" and put themselves in God's hands. Until we step out in faith in the scary areas of our lives, we will never know what God can do.

Your small group will be challenged in this chapter to see where in their lives they can point only to God's power. By encouraging them to move past the safe places into the scary areas of their lives, you will help them discover a bigger God. And that is, after all, the size he really is. We just need to look through eyes of faith in order to accurately see him.

Share

- If you could have seen Jesus do any miracle, which one would you have liked to see? Why?

- Has God ever shown up for you in a dramatic way? If so, when?

- Do you think there is something more Jesus could have done while he was here to prove he was the Son of God? Why/ Why not?

Observe

Observation Questions

- What did Jesus do when he heard what happened to John the Baptist? (verse 13) What did the crowds do?

- How did Jesus feel when he saw the crowds after they followed him? (verse 14) What did he do?

- How many loaves and fish did Jesus use to feed the people? (verse 17) How much was left over? (verse 20) How many were fed? (verse 21)

- Where did the disciples see Jesus in verse 25? What was their response? (verse 26) What did Peter do? (verse 28)

Think

Interpretation Questions

- Why did Herod want to kill John the Baptist? (verses 3-5) What does that tell you about Herod?

- What lesson did the disciples learn about Jesus in verses 15-21?

- Why do you think Jesus walked on water to the disciples? (verses 25-26) How do you think this changed the disciples' view of Jesus?

- Why did Peter start to sink when he was walking on the water? (verse 30) Do you think Peter exercised more faith or less faith than the other disciples?

Apply

Application Questions

- Do miracles strengthen your faith? Why/Why not?

- What is the biggest miracle you have seen God do in your life?

- Where do you need to take a step of faith and "get out of the boat?"

- Is there an area of your life where you need to take your eyes off the storm and put them on Jesus?

Do

Optional Activity

Have your students share one way they can take a step of faith this week and do something they've never done before. After each person shares, have them get into the middle of the circle and have everyone else in the group lay hands on them and pray for them to have the strength to take their step of faith. Ask Jesus to reveal himself as the student steps out in faith. Then come back the following week and share stories.

QUIET TIME REFLECTIONS

Day 1: Matthew 14:1-5

- What word or verse stands out to you from this passage? Why?

- Why did Herod want to kill John the Baptist? Why was he afraid to do it?

- Spend time thinking today about the kind of king Herod was, and how pride leads to fear and control.

Day 2: Matthew 14:6-12

- What word or verse stands out to you from this passage? Why?

- What did Herod promise Herodias' daughter? Why did he fulfill his promise even though it distressed him?

- Spend time thinking today about the things you do to gain approval from others.

Day 3: Matthew 14:13-14

- What word or phrase stands out to you from these verses? Why?

- What did Jesus do when he heard what happened to John the Baptist? How does that speak to you?

- Spend time thinking today about what you do when you get difficult news. Do you turn to God?

Day 4: Matthew 14:15-21

- What word or verse stands out to you from this passage? Why?

- How many loaves and fishes did Jesus use to feed all the people? What does that show you about the way God can provide?

- Spend time thinking today about something you need and how to trust God to provide it.

Day 5: Matthew 14:22-27

- What word or verse stands out to you from this passage? Why?

- How do you think the disciples felt when they first saw Jesus on the lake? How would you have felt?

- Spend time thinking today about your concept of God and how big or small it is. Do you really believe he is Lord of all creation?

Day 6: Matthew 14:28-36

- What word or verse stands out to you from this passage? Why?

- When did Peter start to sink? Where in your life do you need to keep your eyes on Jesus?

- Spend time thinking today about how focusing on God puts into perspective the problems or circumstances you are facing.

Day 7: Matthew 14

Read through the whole chapter and write out the verse that spoke to you most this week. Meditate on that verse today—and for an extra challenge, memorize it!

15. IT'S THE INSIDE THAT COUNTS
Matthew 15

LEADER'S INSIGHT

Have you ever noticed how people's appearances change when you get to know them? People who are attractive on the outside can be downright homely when you get to know them. Conversely, some of the plainest people I know have become the most beautiful over time. We all know that what's inside a person eventually takes over and changes what's on the outside.

And in this chapter, Jesus says the same thing is true about faith.

The Pharisees appeared to be the closest to God by the way they looked. However, when Jesus came, he exposed their hearts. Suddenly what they were like on the inside took over the way they looked. And Jesus let them know he wasn't happy with what he saw.

Later in the chapter, a woman who appeared to be far from God in her social standing ended up being commended by Jesus as having great faith. What was true about her internally took over the way she appeared. When Jesus saw her humble heart, he stopped and healed her daughter. And this encounter changed his (and everyone else's) impression of her.

Your students will see in this chapter that the way they present themselves pales in comparison to what lies within their hearts. Because with Jesus, it's what's on the inside that counts.

Share

- Have you ever had an impression of someone from the outside that changed once you got to know the inside? If so, how did it change?

- Have you ever been desperate for God to answer a prayer? If so, how did it affect your prayer life?

- What lesson or truth does God have to keep teaching you? Is there a lesson you have to keep learning again and again?

Observe

Observation Questions

- How does Jesus answer the Pharisees' question in verses 2-3? What does he say to them in verse 6?

- According to Jesus, what makes people "unclean"? (verse 11) How does he explain it in verses 17-20?

- Why does Jesus grant the request of the woman in verses 25-28? (See verse 27.)

- How many loaves and fish did Jesus use to feed the 4,000? (verse 34) What was left over? (verse 37)

Think

Interpretation Questions

- Why was Jesus mad at the Pharisees in verses 2-9? What was their priority?

- Why does Jesus say a better marker for holiness is what comes out of our mouths rather than what goes in? (verses 16-20) How do you define holiness?

- What do you feel when you read Jesus' encounter in verses 21-28? Does anything confuse you? How do you interpret Jesus' actions?

- Do you think Jesus was frustrated with the disciples in verses 32-33 when you look back at what happened in Chapter 14 (verses 15-21)? What does that tell you about our memory of God's faithfulness?

Apply

Application Questions

- What does being "clean" mean to you? What does being "unclean" mean?

- Have you ever persevered with a prayer request, and saw how God finally answered it? If so, when?

- In what situation have you experienced God's faithfulness in the past that could help you with something you are struggling with right now?

- Which do you need to work on most, your thoughts or your actions? Why?

Do

Optional Activity

Find four photos of beautiful, well-known models or actors (two men, two women) and five pictures of some of the heroes of the faith (e.g., Mother Teresa, Billy Graham, Corrie ten Boom, Dietrich Bonhoeffer). Pass the photos around and have your students choose the four most beautiful. Then have your students choose which have lives that are the most beautiful. Discuss which is more important and why.

QUIET TIME REFLECTIONS

Day 1: Matthew 15:1-6

- What word or verse stands out to you from this passage? Why?

- How does Jesus confront the Pharisees about what is important and what isn't important?

- Spend time today thinking about whether your focus is on following rules or following Jesus.

Day 2: Matthew 15:7-11

- What word or verse stands out to you from this passage? Why?

- According to Jesus, what makes you unclean? What things come out of your mouth?

- Spend time thinking today about what you show about yourself through your speech and actions.

Day 3: Matthew 15:12-20

- What word or verse stands out to you from this passage? Why?

- What are some of the things that come out of people's hearts that make them unclean? Do any of the things on Jesus' list apply to you?

- Spend time thinking today about any sinful thoughts you have and what you can do to replace them with healthy thoughts.

Day 4: Matthew 15:21-28

- What word or verse stands out to you from this passage? Why?

- Why does Jesus grant the Canaanite woman's request? What does that tell you about the importance of faith?

- Spend time thinking today about how much faith you have, and whether you are nurturing your own faith or relying on others' faith.

Day 5: Matthew 15:29-31

- What word or verse stands out to you from this passage? Why?

- What did Jesus do with the great crowds of people? What did the people do when he did it?

- Spend time thinking today about how much you praise God for the things he does. What can you praise him for today?

Day 6: Matthew 15:32-39

- What word or verse stands out to you from this passage? Why?

- Why do you think the disciples wondered how Jesus would provide for the people? What does that tell you about the importance of remembering what God has done?

- Spend time thinking today about how God has provided for you in the past, and how he will provide for you in the future.

Day 7: Matthew 15

Read through the whole chapter and write out the verse that spoke to you most this week. Meditate on that verse today, and for an extra challenge, memorize it!

16. SEEING THROUGH GOD'S EYES
Matthew 16

LEADER'S INSIGHT

Has anyone ever seen something in you before you saw it in yourself? That's what happens to Simon Peter in this chapter. Jesus gives Simon a new name—Peter—to signify that he will be the "rock" of the church. It's something Peter *will* become. But Jesus sees it in him already.

As youth workers, we have that same opportunity: to see in students what they might not yet see in themselves. It means having a "God's-eye view," a perspective that reaches beyond the teenager we see, to the person God is forming. This God's-eye view is developed as we pay attention to where God is and what he is showing us.

Peter had a God's-eye view in this chapter when he saw Jesus for who he really was *("You are the Christ, son of the living God.")*. The Pharisees *didn't* have a God's-eye view, as is apparent in the way they viewed Jesus. They continued to ask for "signs," when the most obvious one was staring them in the face.

A God's-eye view also means we look at things from heaven-down, rather than earth-up. That's what Peter forgot at the end of the chapter. But he and the rest of the disciples eventually saw that though Jesus wasn't the earthly king they imagined; he was the heavenly king that ruled. And his death would be the necessary road to his throne.

Share

- Have you ever wanted a sign from God? Have you ever gotten one?

- Would seeing Jesus change or alter your belief? Do you feel like you have seen enough to have faith in him?

- Do you think you follow God on your terms or his terms? Why?

Observe

Observation Questions

- What is the only sign Jesus said would be given about him? (verse 4)

- What was Jesus' warning in verse 6? According to verse 12, what did the "yeast" of the Pharisees and Sadducees symbolize?

- What did Jesus name Simon? (verse 18) What did his new name mean?

- What does Jesus call Peter in verse 23? What does he say his followers must do in verse 24?

Think

Interpretation Questions

- Why do you think Jesus gives the sign of Jonah as his sign? What are the parallels between Jonah and Jesus?

- Do you understand why the disciples got confused in verse 7? Why do you think Jesus answered the way he did in verse 8?

- Why do you think Jesus says what he says to Peter in verse 17? What does this tell you about sharing your faith? Which part is up to us? Which part is up to God?

- How do you interpret what Jesus says in verses 24-25? What does he mean when he says we need to lose our life in order to save it?

Apply

Application Questions

- If Jesus told you to beware of someone's influence in your life, who would it be?

- Have you ever made a "confession of faith?" If so, when? If not, why not?

- If Jesus gave you an assignment based on something he saw in you, what do you think it would be?

- Would you say you have "lost" your life for Jesus' sake? Why/why not?

Do

Optional Activity

Pass out paper to your group and have them write a new name for the person on their left based on a quality they see in him/her (you can vary who writes for whom depending on your group). Go around and share the new names, and have the group vote on whether to approve or amend the name. Explain how powerful "naming" can be as we see it exemplified in this chapter.

QUIET TIME REFLECTIONS

Day 1: Matthew 16:1-4

- What word or verse stands out to you from this passage? Why?

- What does Jesus say about interpreting signs in this passage? What is the only sign Jesus gives?

- Spend time thinking today about how much you are willing to have faith without signs.

Day 2: Matthew 16:5-7

- What word or verse stands out to you from this passage? Why?

- Why do you think the disciples interpreted Jesus the way they did? How did they miss the mark?

- Spend time thinking today about how we can sometimes misinterpret Scripture and think "on the surface" instead of what the words or images really mean.

Day 3: Matthew 16:8-12

- What word or verse stands out to you from this passage? Why?

- How did Jesus explain what he was actually talking about? Why did he reprimand the disciples about their faith?

- Spend time thinking today about how much faith Jesus would say that you have.

Day 4: Matthew 16:13-20

- What word or verse stands out to you from this passage? Why?

- What does Jesus say about Peter's confession of faith? Who revealed this to Peter?

- Spend time praying for someone you know who doesn't know Christ—that God would open his or her eyes and reveal who he is to him or her.

Day 5: Matthew 16:21-23

- What word or verse stands out to you from this passage? Why?

- What does Jesus call Peter in this passage? What does that tell you about the way Satan works?

- Spend time thinking about how Satan uses people and circumstances to take our focus off God.

Day 6: Matthew 16:24-28

- What word or verse stands out to you from this passage? Why?

- What three things does Jesus say his followers must do? (verse 24) Do you feel like you've done those things? How does the next verse explain what it means to be a believer?

- Spend time thinking today about what it means to lose your life to Christ.

Day 7: Matthew 16

Read through the whole chapter and write out the verse that spoke to you most this week. Meditate on that verse today—and for an extra challenge, memorize it!

17. THINGS TO COME
Matthew 17

LEADER'S INSIGHT

Many of us have a place where God has met us in a special way, where we've experienced his presence more strongly than any other place. God gives us these glimpses to remind us there's more going on than what we see. This chapter shows us three examples of these glimpses.

The first glimpse is the most profound. Known as "The Transfiguration," it's the time when Peter, James, and John see Jesus in a light they've never seen him in before. Watching him speak to Moses and Elijah, the disciples realize they've been given a peek into heaven. Like your students when they have a profound experience with God at a conference or retreat, Peter wants to stay on that mountain forever. But it was just a glimpse—to strengthen and encourage his faith.

Peter and the disciples go on from there to witness Jesus heal a demon-possessed man, and find money for the temple tax in the mouth of a fish—two other events that gave them a glimpse of his deity. But for the disciples—and for us—these are only a foreshadowing of things to come.

One day everyone will see Jesus the way he is seen in this chapter. Until then we live the journey of faith.

Share

- Have you ever experienced a moment that you wish would have lasted forever? If so, when?

- When was the last time you experienced the presence of Jesus? Is there a time or place where you feel especially close to him?

- Have you ever seen something that felt like it was the work of a demon? If so, what did you do?

Observe

Observation Questions

- Who saw Jesus during his transfiguration? (verse 1) Who appeared with Jesus on the mountain? (verse 3)

- What happened in the sky while Peter was speaking in verse 5? How did the disciples react?

- How does Jesus answer the disciples about their inability to drive the demon away? (verses 19-20)

- What does Jesus say is going to happen to him in verses 22-23? How do the disciples respond?

Think

Interpretation Questions

- Why do you think Peter says what he does in verse 4? What does that tell you about the moment he and James and John had on the mountain?

- Why do you think Jesus tells the three disciples not to tell anyone about what they saw? (verse 9) What does this tell you about Jesus?

- Why do you think Jesus got frustrated in verse 17? According to his statements in verse 17 and verse 20, what does he seem to want most from people?

- How do you think the disciples felt when Jesus said what he did in verse 27? Do you think they believed it would be just as he said?

Apply

- Have you ever been some place where God's presence was so strong that you didn't want to leave? If so, where was it?

- Have you ever "seen" God in a way that was hard to explain? If so, when?

- Has there ever been a time when you felt you were being spiritually attacked? If so, what did you do?

- Where do you need more faith right now in your life? How can your belief be strengthened?

Do

Optional Activity

"Faith to move a mountain": Have everyone draw a stick figure on one side of a blank page and a cross on the other side with a mountain in between them. Somewhere on the mountain, have them write down a burden or prayer request that feels impossible. Go around the group and have people share their "mountains," and after they do, have the rest of the group pray Matthew 17-20 into their life. Keep the mountains somewhere where you can retrieve them at a later meeting and see what God has done.

QUIET TIME REFLECTIONS

Day 1: Matthew 17:1-4

- What word or verse stands out to you from this passage? Why?

- What did Peter say when Jesus was transfigured on the mountain? Have you ever been somewhere that the presence of God was so strong you didn't want to leave?

- Spend time thinking today about how God's presence is with us always—we just sometimes have to look harder to see him.

Day 2: Matthew 17:5-8

- What word or verse stands out to you from this passage? Why?

- What happened after the disciples heard God's voice and were terrified? Have you ever been comforted by the presence of Jesus when you were afraid?

- Spend time thinking today about how to focus more on Jesus and less on your fears.

Day 3: Matthew 17:9-13

- What word or verse stands out to you from this passage? Why?

- Who do the disciples think Jesus is comparing Elijah to? In what way was John similar to Elijah? (See 1 Kings 17.)

- Spend time thinking today about the role of prophets in coming before God and speaking for him. Why don't we have prophets today?

Day 4: Matthew 17:14-18

- What word or verse stands out to you from this passage? Why?

- Why do you think Jesus got so upset before he healed the boy? What does that tell you about the way Jesus values faith?

- Spend time thinking today about what you need faith for, and ask God to give you that faith.

Day 5: Matthew 17:19-23

- What word or verse stands out to you from this passage? Why?

- What does Jesus say will happen if we have faith the size of a mustard seed? Do you think that means we get everything we want—or everything we need?

- Spend time thinking today about how God wants to answer your prayers—and you need to trust that he will do it the way he knows is best.

Day 6: Matthew 17:24-27

- What word or verse stands out to you from this passage? Why?

- How does Jesus show he is Lord over everything in this passage?

- Spend time thinking today about the fact that God can do anything! What do you need him to do?

Day 7: Matthew 17

Read through the whole chapter and write out the verse that spoke to you most this week. Meditate on that verse today—and for an extra challenge, memorize it!

18. COMPASSION AND FORGIVENESS
Matthew 18

LEADER'S INSIGHT

Grace is given so that it can be lived. However, we are not always the best dispensers of the grace we've received. We tend to hold our grace in a cup, rather than keep it in a sifter. That's what this chapter is about.

Most of us have no trouble receiving grace. However, when the time comes for us to extend grace, we put conditions on how and when we give it away. But the grace Jesus speaks about in this chapter has no conditions. Since God has given his unmerited grace to us, we have to be willing to do the same for others—whether they deserve it or not. The "not" is the challenge of our faith.

In this chapter, your students will explore their willingness to forgive, and look at where they need to extend grace, even when it is not deserved. There are times when the only motivation we have is the grace we've received from God. But this, Jesus says, should be enough.

In the world we are taught that people need to deserve our forgiveness in order to receive it. But in this chapter, we learn differently. In a system of obedience and reward, grace is a game changer. And God sent his son to show us that we don't need to make the first move toward grace. God already made that move for us.

Now he calls us to do the same for others.

Share

- Which would you hate losing the most, your eyes or your legs? Why?

- Has anyone ever done something to you that was hard to forgive? Without naming names, what was it?

- Has God's forgiveness made a difference in your ability to forgive others? If so, how?

Observe

Observation Questions

- What does Jesus say about sin in verses 8-9? According to his words, which is worse, for us to lose a body part or lose our whole selves?

- According to verse 15, what is the first step we make when we have a problem with someone? What do we do if the person doesn't listen?

- What does Jesus say happens when two or three come together (in verses 19-20)?

- In Jesus' parable in verses 22-34, what happens to the servant who is unable to pay his debt? (verse 27) What does the servant do with the one who owes him a debt? (verse 30) What does the master do when he finds out about the servant's behavior? (verses 32-34)

Think

Interpretation Questions

- Why do you think Jesus says we need to be like children in order to enter the kingdom of heaven? (verse 3) Does verse 4 help clarify what he means?

- What do you think Jesus means in verse 8? Do you think he is speaking literally or figuratively?

- Why do you think Jesus told the Parable of the Lost Sheep in verses 12-14? What point was he trying to make with his audience?

- How do Jesus' words in verses 21-22 relate to his parable in verses 23-35? What is his message about forgiveness in this parable?

Apply

Application Questions

- Is there a part of your body that tends to get you into trouble? If so, what are some things you can do to keep it from leading you into sin?

- Do you relate more to the lost sheep Jesus goes to find, or the 99 who are with Jesus? Why?

- Is there someone you need to have a conversation with who has done something that hurt you? If so, how will you handle it?

- Would you say you are good at forgiving others? Is there someone you might need to forgive? If so, when/how will you do this?

Do

Optional Activity

Pass out slips of paper to everyone in your group. Have everyone write down a person's name (first initial only) whom they need to forgive or who might need to forgive them. Then have them fold their papers and put them in a pile in the middle of the group. Last, have everyone take a piece of paper (if they get their own, have them put it back and choose another one). Then have them pray for their name every day until the group meets again. Share any stories students want to share.

QUIET TIME REFLECTIONS

Day 1: Matthew 18:1-6

- What word or verse stands out to you from this passage? Why?

- What does Jesus say we need to be like to enter the kingdom of heaven? Why do you think he says this?

- Spend time thinking today about how you can be more like a child with your faith.

Day 2: Matthew 18:7-9

- What word or verse stands out to you from this passage? Why?

- What does Jesus say we should do with things that cause us to sin? Is there anything you need to cut off or throw away?

- Spend time thinking today about where you need to focus, and where you need to stay away to keep yourself away from sin.

Day 3: Matthew 18:10-14

- What word or verse stands out to you from this passage? Why?

- What does this parable tell you about the way God cares for those who stray from him? How does that make you feel?

- Spend time thinking today about whether you are the one sheep who has wandered, or part of the 99 sheep who are with Jesus. Either way, God loves you!

Day 4: Matthew 18:15-18

- What word or verse stands out to you from this passage? Why?

- What is the process we are supposed to go through with someone who has wronged us? What do you usually do with someone who has wronged you?

- Spend time thinking today about the way you will handle it next time you have a problem with someone. Is there someone you need to work things out with right now?

Day 5: Matthew 18:19-22

- What word or verse stands out to you from this passage? Why?

- What does Jesus say about prayer and forgiveness in this passage? Which do you need the most help with right now?

- Spend time thinking today about any prayer requests you have. Who might you get to pray with you about it?

Day 6: Matthew 18:23-35

- What word or verse stands out to you from this passage? Why?

- What is the main point of Jesus' parable? How does it speak to you?

- Spend time thinking today about who you need to forgive and ask God for the strength to do it.

Day 7: Matthew 18

Read through the whole chapter and write out the verse that spoke to you most this week. Meditate on that verse today—and for an extra challenge, memorize it!

19. PUTTING GOD FIRST
Matthew 19

LEADER'S INSIGHT

Imagine you are a contestant on *Let's Make a Deal*. In the box, you have your most prized possession. Behind the curtain, there is a ticket to somewhere amazing that you have never been. AND you are promised that your very best friend gets to go with you. You have to trade in the box to get what's behind the curtain. What would you do?

For many of us, the answer to that question depends on our relationship with what's inside the box. That's what your students will wrestle with in this chapter. If they have determined they cannot live without the box, they'll say no to the curtain. And that's a little bit like what happens in this chapter.

It's easy to say God is first. It's another thing to live it. If God is really first, it's reflected in our time, our money, and our relationships. And that's the point Jesus brings home in this chapter. Sometimes it's easier to think about Christianity as following a set of rules. It's a lot riskier to think about it as following a person. But the risk is matched by the guarantee that if we are willing to let go of what we have, we'll get something more than we can imagine. We just have to let go of the box.

This is something the rich man couldn't do. And he missed out on all that waited for him behind the curtain. Sadder still, he walked away from the traveling companion he would have had on his journey.

Share

- Do you tend toward being a rule keeper or a rule breaker? Why?

- When you think about your relationship with God, is it more about following rules or following Jesus? What's the difference?

- If you had to name the one thing that would be hardest to give up, what would it be?

Observe

Observation Questions

- According to Jesus in verse 8, what was the reason Moses permitted divorce? What does Jesus say about divorce in verse 9?

- In verse 14, to whom does Jesus say the kingdom of heaven belongs? What had the disciples done just prior to this? (verse 13)

- How does Jesus respond to the rich man's question in verse 16? Which commandments did the rich man keep? (verse 20) What did he still lack? (verse 21)

- According to verse 22, why did the rich man go away sad? How did the disciples respond? (verse 25) What does Jesus say in verse 26?

Think

Interpretation Questions

- Do you think Jesus strengthened people's view of marriage by what he said in verses 4-9? How do you think marriage was viewed in that culture?

- Why do you think the disciples said what they did in verse 10?

- Do you think the rich man knew something was holding him back when he approached Jesus in verse 16—or do you think he was surprised? Why?

- Why do you think the disciples were so taken aback in verse 25? How do you interpret Jesus' statement in verse 26?

Apply

Application Questions

- Do you feel like you have a good model for what marriage is supposed to be? Why/why not?

- Do you think you will marry someday? If so, do you view this as a permanent commitment? What are some things you could do to prepare yourself for that commitment?

- Would you say God is first in your life? What things in your life reveal that you are a Christian? Are others aware of your commitment?

- If you were to ask Jesus, "What do I still lack?" what do you think he'd say to you? What would be the hardest thing for him to ask you to give up?

Do

Optional Activity

Cut out a cross from poster board, put it on a table and have each person in your group draw a picture or symbol on the cross of whatever is hardest for them to let go of and give to God. After all the pictures/symbols are on the cross, pray as a group (silently or out loud) for your students to give it to God.

QUIET TIME REFLECTIONS

Day 1: Matthew 19:1-6

- What word or verse stands out to you from this passage? Why?

- What does Jesus say happens to a man and woman when they marry? What does that tell you about the seriousness of marriage?

- Spend time praying today for your future spouse. Pray also for yourself to be growing into the best partner you can be for him or her.

Day 2: Matthew 19:7-12

- What word or verse stands out to you from this passage? Why?

- What does Jesus say about divorce in this passage? Do you have anyone close to you who has been affected by divorce?

- Spend time praying today for you or anyone you know who's been affected by the pain of divorce. Pray for healing and strength in that person's brokenness.

Day 3: Matthew 19:13-15

- What word or verse stands out to you from this passage? Why?

- Who does the kingdom of heaven belong to? Why do you think that is?

- Spend time thinking today about Jesus' love for children and how God wants us to retain the innocence of a child.

Day 4: Matthew 19:16-21

- What word or verse stands out to you from this passage? Why?

- What is the one thing the rich man lacks according to Jesus? What do you think Jesus would say to you about what you lack?

- Spend time thinking today about the thing(s) that keep you from being sold out to Christ.

Day 5: Matthew 19:22-26

- What word or verse stands out to you from this passage? Why?

- Who does Jesus say makes it possible for a rich man (or anyone else) to enter heaven? Why do you think we need God's help?

- Spend time thinking today about where you need God's help in letting go of something to follow him.

Day 6: Matthew 19:27-30

- What word or verse stands out to you from this passage? Why?

- What will we receive if we are willing to leave everything for Christ? How does that make you feel?

- Spend time thinking today about what we will gain for eternity if we are willing to give up the things we cling to here.

Day 7: Matthew 19

Read through the whole chapter and write out the verse that spoke to you most this week. Meditate on that verse today—and for an extra challenge, memorize it!

20. FAIRNESS AND GRACE
Matthew 20

LEADER'S INSIGHT

How would you feel if you worked a whole day, and another person came and worked for the last hour and got paid as much as you? Most of us would scream (out loud or in our minds), "That's not fair!" And we'd be right.

Jesus clearly illustrates in this chapter that grace isn't fair. But ironically, the unfairness of grace is also its greatest asset. Think about it—do we really want fairness when it comes to God's grace? If we got what we deserved from God, we would all be dead. That's the punishment our sins deserve. Instead, God has given us what we *don't* deserve—an opportunity for life. And whether we receive this gift when we are children or on our deathbeds, it's ours. It doesn't increase or decrease according to the amount of our works.

In this chapter, your students will see (and experience) what the unfairness of grace really means. It's a lesson we all need to remember when it comes to our faith. Otherwise, we quickly resort to a relationship with God that's based on a system of obedience and reward. Like James and John illustrate in this chapter, sometimes when we're obedient to God, we believe he owes us more. But Jesus shows us clearly in this chapter that's not the way God works.

Ultimately, we will thank him for it.

Share

Warm-Up Questions

- Is it hard for you to show grace to people who don't deserve it? Why/Why not?

- Would you describe God as fair or unfair? Why?

- Have you ever wanted to "share the limelight" with someone who was getting attention? If so, when?

Observe

Observation Questions

- In the Parable of the Vineyard, how many times did the landowner go out to find workers? (verses 3, 5-6) What times during the day did he go out? How much did he pay each of them? (verses 8-9)

- How did the landowner respond when the workers complained? (verses 13-15)

- What did the mother of Zebedee's sons (James and John) ask Jesus? (verse 21) What was his response? (verse 23) How did the other disciples react to this request? (verse 24)

- What did Jesus say to the blind men who cried for mercy? (verse 32) What did he do next? (verse 34)

Think

Interpretation Questions

- Why do you think Jesus told the Parable of the Vineyard? What do you think he was trying to communicate about grace?

- Do you think the workers who came early were justified in their complaint? Why/Why not?

- What does Jesus say about the way to be a leader in verses 25-26? How did he model this?

- Why do you think Jesus asked the blind men what they

wanted him to do? Do you think it was obvious? What purpose do you think he had in asking them?

Apply

Application Questions

- How would you have felt if you were one of the early vineyard workers in Jesus' parable? Do you think Jesus is being
  fair to them?

- Is it harder for you to accept God's grace in your life—or
  in others' lives? Do you ever feel like his grace should be
  limited?

- Where in your life do you have the opportunity to serve others? What could you do this week to serve someone?

- If Jesus asked what you wanted him to do for you right now,
  what would you say?

Do

Optional Activity

Create a small obstacle course that your students have to go through,
and tell them the first two people who make it through get an ice
cream sundae. (You can use cookies if it's easier.) When the first
two students finish, give them their prize. Then after the rest of the
students finish, give them all the same prize. Ask the students who
came in first how they felt about the others getting this same prize.
Ask the students who came in last how they felt. Draw analogies
between this exercise and the Parable of the Vineyard.

QUIET TIME REFLECTIONS

Day 1: Matthew 20:1-7

- What word or verse stands out to you from this passage? Why?
- How many different times did the landowner go out to find workers? What does that tell you about how God pursues us?
- Spend time thinking today about when you responded to God's call. If you haven't yet, why not do it today?

Day 2: Matthew 20:8-16

- What word or verse stands out to you from this passage? Why?
- How much did all the workers get paid? What does that tell you about God's timing and grace?
- Spend time thinking today about the unfairness of grace, and thank God for it.

Day 3: Matthew 20:17-19

- What word or phrase stands out to you from this passage? Why?
- What does Jesus tell the disciples in this passage? Do you think they understood what he was saying?
- Spend time thinking today about how Jesus' purpose on earth was to die for our sins and give us new life. Praise him for what he was willing to go through on your behalf!

Day 4: Matthew 20:20-23

- What word or verse stands out to you from this passage? Why?
- Why do you think James and John's mother asked Jesus what she did? What does that tell you about what she wanted for her sons?
- Spend time thinking today about how your mom wants the

best for you, even if she sometimes goes about it the wrong way.

Day 5: Matthew 20:24-28

- What word or verse stands out to you from this passage? Why?

- What does Jesus teach the disciples about power and leadership in this passage? Where in your life can you practice servant leadership?

- Spend time thinking today about some ways you could be a servant. Is there anything you can do to serve someone today?

Day 6: Matthew 20:29-34

- What word or verse stands out to you from this passage? Why?

- Why do you think Jesus asked the blind men what they wanted? Wasn't it obvious? What was his purpose in asking?

- Spend time today thinking about how Jesus wants to know what we want before he gives it to us. That's why we pray!

Day 7: Matthew 20

Read through the whole chapter and write out the verse that spoke to you most this week. Meditate on that verse today—and for an extra challenge, memorize it!

21. FAN OR FOLLOWER?
Matthew 21

LEADER'S INSIGHT

If you are a sports lover, you know there are two different groups who show up at a game. Fans are the ones who are there to cheer for their team as long as they win. Followers are the ones who cheer for their team no matter how far behind they get. Fans quickly get on board when their team is having a winning streak, but they just as quickly bail when the going gets tough. Followers show up in the rain, even if their team looks like they might end up in last place.

When it comes to Jesus, are you more of a fan or a follower? In this chapter, your students will see the difference. The chapter opens with the most popular event of Jesus' ministry, where fans and followers show up to cheer him. Jesus was at the top of his game, and it seemed like he was going places. However the fans slowly faded away as they learned where Jesus was headed. And they disappeared when he was nailed to a cross.

But Jesus doesn't seem to care much about fans. What he wants are followers. After the triumphal entry, he doesn't bask in his popularity. Instead he heads to the temple and knocks down the tables of moneychangers. Right after that, he tells two parables that accuse the Pharisees of "not getting it" when it comes to God. With each successive event, his popularity takes a downgrade as the chapter closes.

But popularity is not what Jesus is after. Commitment is.

Share

- When it comes to Jesus, would you say you were more of a fan or a follower? Why?

- Who is the most famous person you have ever seen? What was it like when you saw him/her?

- Do you tend to make commitments quickly and sometimes retract them—or do you wait to commit until you've thought about it?

Observe

Observation Questions

- What prophecy was fulfilled when Jesus came into Jerusalem on a donkey? (verse 5)

- What did Jesus do when he entered the temple area? (verse 12) What did he say? (verse 13)

- Which of the sons in the Parable of the Two Sons did what his father wanted? What analogy does Jesus draw from this parable in verses 31-32?

- In the Parable of the Tenants, what happened to the land-owner's servants? (verses 35-36) What happened to his son? (verses 38-39) What Scripture does Jesus quote after telling this parable? (verse 42)

Think

Interpretation Questions

- Do you think Jesus looked like a king when he rode into Jerusalem? (verses 6-9) Why/Why not? Why didn't he choose another approach?

- Why do you think Jesus got so irate at the moneychangers in the temple? Do you think what they were doing was that bad?

- Why do you think Jesus answered the question about his

authority the way he did? (verses 23-27) What does this show you about Jesus?

- In Jesus' Parable of the Tenants, whom do you think the landowner symbolizes? How about the tenants? The servants? The son? What point was Jesus trying to make by telling this parable?

Apply

Application Questions

- Based on your relationship with Jesus right now, do you think you would be a disciple, a Pharisee, or a distant part of the audience at the triumphal entry? Why?

- According to Jesus' actions in the temple (verses 12-13), what things should make us angry today? What do you think God wants us to do about it?

- In your commitment to Christ, are you more like the first son or the second son in Jesus' parable in verses 28-32? Why?

- What do we learn from some of the issues Jesus had with the religious people? Is there a warning for us as Christians today? If so, what is it?

Do

Optional Activity

Take a poster board and put at the top the words "Fan" and "Follower." Divide a line down the middle so you have two columns underneath these words. Have your students come up with words or phrases that describe what a person's life is like when he or she is a Fan of Jesus, and what his or her life is like when he or she is a Follower. What are the differences? Any similarities? Which list best describes your students?

QUIET TIME REFLECTIONS

Day 1: Matthew 21:1-11

- What word or verse stands out to you from this passage? Why?

- What prophecy did Jesus fulfill by riding into Jerusalem on a donkey? (See Zechariah 9:9.) What did the crowd do?

- Spend time thinking today about whether you are more of a fan or follower of Jesus. Which would you like to be?

Day 2: Matthew 21:12-22

- What word or verse stands out to you from this passage? Why?

- How does Jesus show his ability to do the impossible in this passage? Does that encourage you to pray more?

- Spend time praying today about something that feels impossible, and ask God for the strength to believe he can do something about it.

Day 3: Matthew 21:23-27

- What word or verse stands out to you from this passage? Why?

- How does Jesus show his intelligence in this passage? What do you think the Pharisees felt?

- Spend time thinking today about Jesus' quiet confidence about who he is. How can that help you know how to defend your faith?

Day 4: Matthew 21:28-32

- What word or verse stands out to you from this passage? Why?

- Are you more like the first son or the second son right now in your faith?

- Spend time thinking today about how God values our actions more than our words.

Day 5: Matthew 21:33-41

- What word or verse stands out to you from this passage? Why?

- Why do you think Jesus tells this parable? What message is he trying to give?

- Spend time thinking today about how God wants us to live until Jesus comes back, and then how he wants us to receive him when he does.

Day 6: Matthew 21:42-45

- What word or verse stands out to you from this passage? Why?

- Who is "the stone the builders rejected"? What did he become?

- Spend time thinking today about how Jesus gave many clues about who he was and what he was doing. How can you listen more carefully to God?

Day 7: Matthew 21

Read through the whole chapter and write out the verse that spoke to you most this week. Meditate on that verse today—and for an extra challenge, memorize it!

22. THE INVITATION
Matthew 22

LEADER'S INSIGHT

Have you ever gotten an invitation and planned to go, but then declined because you got a better offer? Or maybe you got so busy that you forgot to attend? I know I have. And there have been times when I've really regretted it. Especially when I heard afterward what I missed.

In this chapter, Jesus describes the life he offers as an invitation. We can say "yes" or "no," but it's up to us to respond. Only by saying "yes" and following through with our response will we be included as his guest. But as we see from the parable in this chapter, the invitation keeps getting extended. And the only people who are denied are the ones who keep themselves away.

This is a great image to remember when it comes to responding to God. And there are descriptions in this chapter of what life is like when we say yes. We learn that relationships in eternity will be different than the ones we have here on earth. But Jesus also has something to say about how to live while we *are* on earth—and he boils it down to two commandments. We are to love God and love our neighbor—and when we do, the rest of the commandments naturally fall into place.

The invitation God gives us extends into eternity. But it has implications here and now. In this lesson, your students will have a chance to think about what life might be like after they leave this earth. But they will also be encouraged to think about what life should be like here and now.

Share

- What is the greatest invitation you ever received? What made it so great?

- How do you picture heaven? Why do you picture it that way?

- Which of God's commandments (that you know) is the hardest for you to follow? Which is the easiest?

Observe

Observation Questions

- Where were the servants sent first in the Parable of the Wedding Banquet? (verse 3) How did they respond? (verses 5-6) Where did the servants go next? (verse 10)

- How did Jesus respond to the question about paying taxes? (verses 19-21) What did Jesus know about the people who asked him this question? (verse 18)

- What does Jesus say about marriage in the Resurrection? (verse 30)

- How many commandments does Jesus name as the greatest? What are they? (verses 37-39)

Think

Interpretation Questions

- Why do you think Jesus told the Parable of the Wedding Banquet? What point was he trying to make?

- Why do you think the Pharisees were amazed by Jesus' answer about paying taxes? (verses 21-22)

- What does Jesus imply about Abraham, Isaac, and Jacob in verses 31-32? What hint does that give you about the afterlife?

- Why do you think Jesus asks the Pharisees whose son the

Christ is? (verse 41) How do you think they interpreted what he said in verses 44-45?

Apply

Application Questions

- What message do you get out of the Parable of the Wedding Banquet? How does it apply to your life right now?

- Do you think we should have to pay taxes when all we have is from God? Why/Why not?

- How do you picture relationships in heaven? In what way are they different or similar to our relationships on earth?

- Why do you think we refer to Jesus as the "Son of David?" How can he be both the Son of David and the Son of God?

Do

Optional Activity

"Your picture of heaven": Give out blank pieces of paper (or poster paper) with markers. (You can grab some magazines and scissors if you want instead.) Tell the students they have 10-15 minutes to draw (or cut and paste) pictures that represent their picture of heaven. At the end, have them share their pictures and explain why it represents their view of what heaven is like.

QUIET TIME REFLECTIONS

Day 1: Matthew 22:1-5

- What word or verse stands out to you from this passage? Why?
- How did the people who were invited respond when the servant came to get them? What were their excuses?
- Spend time thinking today about the excuses you've given God. What might he be inviting you to do today?

Day 2: Matthew 22:6-14

- What word or verse stands out to you from this passage? Why?
- Who got invited to the banquet? What do you think the "wedding clothes" symbolized that caused the man to be thrown out?
- Spend time thinking today about what is required to go to God's banquet. What is God's part? What is our part?

Day 3: Matthew 22:15-22

- What word or verse stands out to you from this passage? Why?
- How does Jesus answer the question about taxes? What does that show you about his wisdom?
- Spend time thinking today about the great teacher Jesus is, and how you can learn from him.

Day 4: Matthew 22:23-33

- What word or verse stands out to you from this passage? Why?
- What does Jesus say about our relationships in heaven? How are they different than our relationships on earth?
- Spend time thinking today about how your relationships will be different in heaven. Pray for those whom you want to be in your family in heaven.

Day 5: Matthew 22:34-40

- What word or verse stands out to you from this passage? Why?

- What are the two greatest commandments? How are they related?

- Spend time today thinking of one way you can love God, and one way you can love your neighbor.

Day 6: Matthew 22:41-46

- What word or verse stands out to you from this passage? Why?

- How can Jesus be David's son and Lord? How does this show his earthly and heavenly side?

- Spend time thinking today about how Jesus was both man and God. Is that hard or easy for you to comprehend?

Day 7: Matthew 22

Read through the whole chapter and write out the verse that spoke to you most this week. Meditate on that verse today—and for an extra challenge, memorize it!

23. SEVEN WOES
Matthew 23

LEADER'S INSIGHT

Do you remember the last time you got into trouble? It may have been a while for you, but your students will likely have a recent memory. And there's a good possibility that their consequences were accompanied by a lecture from their parent or teacher. Most of your students will agree that the worst kind of lecture is one that happens in front of other people. And that's a little bit like what happens in this chapter.

Commonly known as the "Seven Woes" chapter, you get the feeling right away that Jesus has had it. And he lets the Pharisees have it for the way they've behaved. Even worse, he does it in front of everyone. He wants to make it perfectly clear that the Pharisees are giving others a bad example of what it means to love God. He also wants to give them one more chance to turn it around before he heads to the cross.

So what are the things in this chapter that Jesus is so mad about? Ultimately the Pharisees were concerned about how religious they looked. But Jesus makes it clear what really matters is the state of your relationship with him. Looking good doesn't amount to much when you're a "whitewashed tomb." It's what's *inside* you that counts.

In this chapter we see that underneath the harshness of truth is the sacrifice of love it takes to speak it. For parents it's the loss of momentary affection. For Jesus it was his life.

Share

Warm-Up Questions

- When you think about hypocrisy, what image comes to your mind?

- Do you think God cares more about following rules or showing mercy? Why?

- When you see someone profess Christianity but act in an unloving way, how does it affect your faith (if at all)?

Observe

Observation Questions

- According to Jesus, what is the Pharisees' motivation for their religious acts? (verse 5) What do verses 6 and 7 say they love?

- What are the first three woes Jesus gives? (verses 13, 15-16) What despairing words does Jesus say about the Pharisees' converts in verse 15?

- What is Jesus' fourth woe? (verse 23) What does he say the Pharisees should have done?

- What are Jesus' last three woes? (verses 25, 27, 29) Make a list (as a group) of all seven woes listed in this chapter.

Think

Interpretation Questions

- Look at what Jesus calls the Pharisees in verse 16. Why do you think he calls them that?

- According to what Jesus says in verse 23, are we supposed to just practice justice, mercy, and faithfulness and not worry about tithing? Why/Why not?

- Why does Jesus say cleaning the inside of the cup cleans the outside? (verse 26) What does he mean?

- After reading Jesus' words in this chapter, do you think we can see how righteous a person is? If so, how?

Apply

Application Questions

- Which of the things Jesus condemns in this chapter do you struggle with the most?

- When you think of an image of a "good Christian," whom do you picture? Why?

- If Jesus were to list some of his woes to Christians today, what do you think they would be?

- If Jesus were to confront you on something you are doing—or not doing—what do you think it would be?

Do

Optional Activity

As a group, make a list of the top seven woes you think Jesus would have for the church today. You can divide your group to come up with one each and then compile the list, or just do it as a group activity. Keep it as a warning for your group to look at periodically and check themselves against.

QUIET TIME REFLECTIONS

Day 1: Matthew 23:1-8

- What word or verse stands out to you from this passage? Why?

- What is Jesus' warning to his disciples about the Pharisees? Why doesn't he want his followers to model themselves after them?

- Spend time today thinking about people who are good models of the faith, and people who aren't. Find a mentor you can look up to as you grow in Christ.

Day 2: Matthew 23:9-12

- What word or verse stands out to you from this passage? Why?

- Who will be exalted and who will be humbled? What does that tell you about the way Jesus wants us to act?

- Spend time thinking today about how you can be more humble. How will you do that?

Day 3: Matthew 23:13-22

- What word or verse stands out to you from this passage? Why?

- What does Jesus speak out against in this passage?

- Spend time thinking today about how Jesus wants us to act as Christians, and how he doesn't want us to act.

Day 4: Matthew 23:23-28

- What word or verse stands out to you from this passage? Why?

- What are we supposed to clean—the inside or the outside? How do we do that?

- Spend time thinking today about what it means to clean the inside of your cup.

Day 5: Matthew 23:29-36

- What word or verse stands out to you from this passage? Why?

- What does Jesus speak out against in this passage?

- Spend time thinking today about how you can avoid being a hypocrite in your faith.

Day 6: Matthew 23:37-38

- What word or phrase stands out to you from this passage? Why?

- Why is Jesus so sad about Jerusalem? To whom is he referring?

- Spend time today thinking about how the people we are closest to have the power to evoke great joy or great sadness because we care so much about them.

Day 7: Matthew 23

Read through the whole chapter and write out the verse that spoke to you most this week. Meditate on that verse today—and for an extra challenge, memorize it!

24. THE END OF THE WORLD
Matthew 24

LEADER'S INSIGHT

I don't know about you, but I'm usually skeptical of end time prophecies. There have been hundreds of them that have come and gone, and since we're still here, it's hard not to be skeptical. The funny thing is, Jesus knew this was going to happen, and that's one of the things he talks about in this chapter. Jesus does have some things to say about the end of the world, but there are also a lot of things he *doesn't* say—like when the end is going to be.

The need to control our destiny has driven many people to study this chapter and try to make parallels with events currently taking place in history. That often leads to a prophecy or prediction for when the end will be. However, Jesus makes it clear in this chapter that NO ONE (including himself) knows the day or the hour.

But that doesn't seem to stop us from trying.

What Jesus *does* indicate in this chapter is that we should spend less time figuring out when the end is going to happen, and more time on what we should be doing when it does. That's what your students will talk about as you study Jesus' words. Since most young people have the mindset that they have forever to change their course, it's good for them to realize that one day the end will come. And that's what this chapter helps us do.

There are signs Jesus gives us in this chapter for when that day will happen. But like Old Testament prophecies, those signs will only fully be interpreted when we look back. The point is, it's going to happen—and whether it happens in two days or two thousand years, our job is not to guess when it will be. Our job is to be ready when it does.

Share

- If someone asked you when you thought the world was going to end, what would you say? Why?

- Have you ever heard a prophecy or theory about the end of the world? If so, when was it?

- What do you think it will be like when Jesus comes again? Do you think it will be similar or different than the way he came before? Why?

Observe

Observation Questions

- What does Jesus say about the signs of his coming in verses 5-8?

- What does Jesus say will happen to believers in verses 9-12? Who will be saved? (verse 13)

- According to verse 30, how will the Son of Man appear? What will he do? (verse 31)

- What does Jesus say about the second coming in verse 36? What warning does he give in verses 23 and 26? What does he say about our readiness in verse 44?

Think

Interpretation Questions

- Why do you think Jesus warns us repeatedly not to be deceived by false prophecies about his coming? (verses 4, 23, 26)

- Look at verse 24. Do you think this has already happened? If so, when have you seen it happen?

- How do you interpret what Jesus says in verses 32-35? How does verse 36 help us not get carried away with prophecies about the end of the world?

- What encouragement does Jesus give us in verses 45-47? What warning does he give us in verses 49-50? What do you think he is calling his followers to do?

Apply

Application Questions

- Have you seen examples of what Jesus talks about in verses 4-8? If so, when?

- How do you feel when you read Jesus' words about the end of the world? Excited? Scared? Hopeful? Anxious? Why?

- Do verses 42-44 inspire you to do anything you are not doing? Or would you feel ready if Christ came back today?

- If you knew the world was going to end tomorrow, what would you do today?

Do

Optional Activity

Pass out paper or index cards, and have your students write at the top "My Last Day." Then have them make a schedule for what they would do if they found out the world was going to end tomorrow and this was their last day. Have everyone share their Last Day Schedules with the rest of the group. Is there anything on their list that they should do now?

QUIET TIME REFLECTIONS

Day 1: Matthew 24:1-8

- What word or verse stands out to you from this passage? Why?

- What does Jesus say will happen before the end of the age? Have you seen any of these things?

- Spend time thinking today about how many of Jesus' words have come to pass.

Day 2: Matthew 24:9-14

- What word or verse stands out to you from this passage? Why?

- What does Jesus say will happen to us? How does that make you feel?

- Spend time today praying for your faith to be strengthened to face any adversity.

Day 3: Matthew 24:15-25

- What word or verse stands out to you from this passage? Why?

- How does Jesus say we are to respond to prophecies about the end of the world?

- Spend time thinking today about how to stay steady in your faith, and not worry about when the end will come.

Day 4: Matthew 24:26-34

- What word or verse stands out to you from this passage? Why?

- How will we be able to know that Jesus is returning? Where will he appear?

- Spend time thinking today about what it will be like when Jesus comes again.

Day 5: Matthew 24:35-44

- What word or verse stands out to you from this passage? Why?

- What does Jesus say about our readiness when he comes? Would you be ready if he came today?

- Spend time today thinking about your readiness to see Christ again.

Day 6: Matthew 24:45-51

- What word or verse stands out to you from this passage? Why?

- What does Jesus warn against in this passage?

- Spend time thinking today about how you can persevere in your faith and grow closer to Christ.

Day 7: Matthew 2

Read through the whole chapter and write out the verse that spoke to you most this week. Meditate on that verse today—and for an extra challenge, memorize it!

25. HE WILL COME
Matthew 25

LEADER'S INSIGHT

This is the only chapter in Matthew that is comprised solely of parables. Jesus tells three stories in a row to emphasize the things we are supposed to be doing before he comes back. The point of each of his parables can be summed up in three phrases: Be ready, use your gifts wisely, love well. But it's the way Jesus tells his stories that make the lessons come alive.

To encourage us to be ready for his coming, Jesus gives us the image of a virgin waiting for her bridegroom. With the excitement of a new bride, we should have our lanterns filled and ready for when the groom arrives to take us to our new home. Then, to encourage us to use our gifts wisely, Jesus tells a story about three servants who are given talents, and what they did with those talents while their master was away. In this parable, we learn that it's not what we have that is most important, but what we *do* with what we have.

Finally, Jesus tells a frightening story to urge us to live a life of love. It's about two groups of people who have opposite responses to people in need, and what ultimately happens to them. To the group who had compassion, he tells them that in serving others, they were serving him. To the group who didn't have compassion, he lets them know their hardheartedness had implications beyond the people they ignored.

By telling stories, Jesus communicates truth in a compelling way that reaches into the heart of his listeners. After studying the truths of Jesus' stories in this chapter, your students will have a chance to do that, too.

Share

Warm-Up Questions

- Have you ever been jolted or surprised by something you didn't expect to happen? If so, when?

- If someone asked you what your greatest talent was, what would you say? Are you using it?

- Have you ever experienced the presence of God in another person? If so, when?

Observe

Observation Questions

- In the Parable of the Ten Virgins, what did the foolish ones do? (verse 3) What did the wise ones do? (verse 4) What happened when the foolish virgins left to get more oil? (verse 10)

- In the Parable of the Talents, how many talents did each servant receive? (verses 15, 17-18) How many did each one end up with?

- What did Jesus say to the first two servants? (verses 21-22) What did he say to the third one? (verses 26-27)

- What happens to the sheep in Jesus' third parable? (verses 34-36) What do they ask Jesus in verses 27-29? How does he answer? (verse 40)

Think

Interpretation Questions

- Who do you think the bridegroom represents in the Parable of the Ten Virgins? (verses 1-13) How about the virgins? What is the point of the parable?

- Do you think the point of Jesus' second parable has to do with the amount of talents we are given or how we use them? What is the lesson that comes from this parable?

- What does verse 40 say about what happens when we care for others? Where does Jesus indicate that he dwells?

- According to this parable, how important is it to Jesus that his followers care for others? Do you think it's possible to be a Christian and not do it? Why/Why not?

Apply

Application Questions

- At this time, would you say you are ready or not ready for Jesus' return? Why?

- In the Parable of the Talents (verses 14-30), are you more like the servant with the five talents, two talents, or one talent? Why?

- When you read the story of The Sheep and the Goats (verses 31-46) how does it make you feel? Why?

- Of the three stories Jesus tells in this chapter, which of them hits home the most for you right now? Why?

Do

Optional Activity

Jesus tells three parables in this chapter, and he does this when he is trying to make a point, or teach something about the way God works. Come up with a couple of topics (God's grace, God's love, forgiveness, giving to others, not showing partiality, etc.) and put the topics in the middle of the circle. Get students in pairs or teams of three, and have them draw one, and give them five minutes to come up with a parable. Then share them at the end.

QUIET TIME REFLECTIONS

Day 1: Matthew 25:1-13

- What word or verse stands out to you from this passage? Why?

- What lesson do you learn from the wise virgins? Is there anything you need to do to be ready for the bridegroom when he comes?

- Spend time thinking today about the things you can do to stay faithful until Christ returns.

Day 2: Matthew 25:14-23

- What word or verse stands out to you from this passage? Why?

- What lesson do you learn from the first two servants in this parable?

- Spend time thinking today about how to use your talents and gifts wisely for God.

Day 3: Matthew 25:24-30

- What word or verse stands out to you from this passage? Why?

- What lesson do you learn from the third servant about what not to do with your talent?

- Spend time thinking today about any talents or gifts you might be burying. How can you use them for God?

Day 4: Matthew 25:31-36

- What word or verse stands out to you from this passage? Why?

- Why does the king commend the sheep in this parable?

- Spend time thinking today about the way you treat the poor. What could you do to help someone in need?

Day 5: Matthew 25:37-40

- What word or verse stands out to you from this passage? Why?

- According to this parable, who are we caring for when we care for the poor? How does that make you feel?

- Spend time thinking today about how Jesus is in those who are in need around you. How does that change the way you see them?

Day 6: Matthew 25:41-46

- What word or verse stands out to you from this passage? Why?

- Why were the goats condemned? Are you more like a sheep or a goat right now in the way you care for people in need?

- Spend time thinking today about what needs to change in your life for you to be more concerned about people in need.

Day 7: Matthew 25

Read through the whole chapter and write out the verse that spoke to you most this week. Meditate on that verse today—and for an extra challenge, memorize it!

26. PREPARATION FOR DEATH
Matthew 26:1-30

LEADER'S INSIGHT

In the first half of Matthew 26, we see the deliberate way Jesus prepares for what he knows is about to happen. Looking back on these events, we can see there was purpose in everything he did. The rearview mirror is the best place to look when we want to see the way God works.

For the disciples, the trip to Simon's house in Bethany was just another stop on their journey with Jesus. But Jesus knew it was one of his last stops before he would head to the cross. With this backdrop, we understand Jesus' anointing by the woman from an entirely different perspective.

We can imagine the awkwardness of the room when this woman began such a personal act. However, Jesus absorbs this embarrassment by not only accepting her actions, but also commending them. The woman moves from disdain to honor with a swift sweep of Jesus' words. And looking back, we understand what she did from a much broader viewpoint. Hopefully your students will too.

Jesus moves from this unusual event to a meal with his disciples, and there he gives new significance to elements they've ingested many times before. Since then, followers throughout history have taken these elements because of what happened at this supper. But I'm fairly sure the disciples had no idea at the time how significant this meal with Jesus would prove to be. That's the God of the rearview mirror.

Share

Warm-Up Questions

- If you had one day left to live, whom would you spend it with? Why?

- What is the hardest time you've gone through (so far) in your faith? What made it difficult?

- Have you ever been with someone who was going through a difficult time? If so, what did you do?

Observe

Observation Questions

- What did the chief priests plan to do with Jesus? (verse 4) Why did they want to wait to do it? (verse 5)

- When the woman anoints Jesus with perfume in verse 7, what do the disciples say? (verses 8-9) How does Jesus respond? (verses 10-13)

- What does Jesus say to his disciples when they are having the last supper? (verse 21) How does he identify who he's talking about?

- What does Jesus say about the bread and the cup? (verses 26-28) What does he say about himself in verse 29?

Think

Interpretation Questions

- Why do you think the chief priests wanted to arrest Jesus in some sly way instead of just going after him? (verse 4) What does that tell you about Jesus?

- Why did Jesus commend the woman who anointed him with perfume? Why do you think her action was so significant?

- When Jesus told the disciples that one of them would betray him, do you think he had a purpose for doing that? Why didn't he just say who it was?

- What do you imagine the disciples were thinking when Jesus was talking about the bread and the cup? (verses 26-27) Do you think they understood what he was saying? What does Jesus mean when he says what he does in verse 29?

Apply

Application Questions

- How do you think you would have felt if you saw the woman anoint Jesus the way she did? (verses 6-8) Can you relate to what the disciples said?

- Do you ever think we overspend our money on buildings of worship when we should be giving more to the poor? How do you think Jesus feels? Do you think it is similar to the perfume anointing in this chapter?

- Do you think Judas had a choice of whether or not to betray Jesus? Or was he forced to follow a preordained script?

- Do you think the disciples understood the significance of Jesus' words in verses 26-28? How do we experience that significance today?

Do

Optional Activity

Take communion together as a group using the words of Jesus from this passage. (If your tradition doesn't allow you to take communion without a pastor, perhaps you can get someone to come for the last 10 minutes of your group.) If you have more flexibility, try passing it around the circle, giving each student an opportunity to repeat Jesus' words as the next student takes the elements.

QUIET TIME REFLECTIONS

Day 1: Matthew 26:1-5

- What word or verse stands out to you from this passage? Why?

- How does Jesus communicate to the disciples once more what's going to happen? Why do you think he does this?

- Spend time thinking today about how Jesus was Lord over all that happened to him. How does that make you feel about what he did?

Day 2: Matthew 26:6-9

- What word or verse stands out to you from this passage? Why?

- What does the woman do for Jesus in this passage? What do you think motivated her to sacrifice her perfume in this way?

- Spend time thinking today about the ways you show Jesus your love. How can you show him your love today?

Day 3: Matthew 26:10-13

- What word or verse stands out to you from this passage? Why?

- What does Jesus say about what the woman has done? How has this come true?

- Spend time thinking today about how important the things we do for Jesus are in the big picture of our lives.

Day 4: Matthew 26:14-16

- What word or verse stands out to you from this passage? Why?

- What sad thing happens in this passage?

- Spend time thinking today about any temptations you may face that could cause you to betray Jesus.

Day 5: Matthew 26:17-25

- What word or verse stands out to you from this passage? Why?

- How does Jesus tell the disciples about Judas? Why doesn't he tell them outright?

- Spend time thinking today about how God wants us to take responsibility for our actions and ask forgiveness when we do something wrong.

Day 6: Matthew 26:26-30

- What word or verse stands out to you from this passage? Why?

- What does Jesus say about the bread and the cup? When was the last time you took communion?

- Spend time thinking today about the significance of communion. Thank Jesus for giving us these elements to remember him.

Day 7: Matthew 26:1-30

Read through the whole chapter and write out the verse that spoke to you most this week. Meditate on that verse today—and for an extra challenge, memorize it!

27. LOYALTY TESTED
Matthew 26:31-75

LEADER'S INSIGHT

Have you ever experienced a downgrade in someone's reputation that made you want to distance yourself from him or her? If it's a good friend, you feel conflict because you want to stand by their side, but you know your reputation will take a hit if you do that. That's a little bit of what the disciples experience in Matthew 26.

In the last half of this chapter, they are confronted with the reality of what Jesus warned them about all along: Jesus will not be taking a throne; he will be taken to a cross. Yet when it starts to happen, the disciples suddenly realize it's going to have implications for *them*— and they are not prepared for the new role they are suddenly forced to take.

By studying these last events of Jesus' life, your students will have an opportunity to look not only at their loyalty to others, but to God. It's easy to stick with someone when he or she is doing what you want. It's not so easy to stick with someone who's doing what you *don't* want him or her to do. And this is true about our relationship with God.

In this chapter, Jesus reveals that he is not the kind of king the disciples thought they wanted. But he *is* the kind of king the disciples will soon realize they need. Our loyalty to God can be tested when we have to lay aside what we want and trust that he's giving us what we need. But in time, we will see why.

Share

Warm-Up Questions

- Have you ever betrayed or let down a good friend? If so, how did it feel?

- Have you ever done something you regretted after you did it? If so, what was it?

- If someone told you he was sent from God, how would you respond?

Observe

Observation Questions

- What does Peter promise Jesus in verse 33? How does Jesus respond? (verse 34) What does Peter say after that?

- What does Jesus ask the disciples to do in verse 36? What do they do? (verse 40) How does Jesus' prayer change between verse 39 and verse 42?

- What happens when Jesus is arrested in verse 51? What does Jesus say in verses 52-54?

- How does Jesus respond when they ask him if he is the Christ? (verses 63-64) What happens to Peter after Jesus is arrested? (verses 69-75)

Think

Interpretation Questions

- Why do you think Jesus tells Peter he will disown him? Do you think he did it for a reason?

- Why do you think Jesus prayed in the garden for the cup to be removed? (verse 39) What does that tell you about Jesus? What does the caveat he added at the end (and then repeated in verse 42) tell us about prayer?

- What does verse 56 tell you about how the disciples felt when Jesus was arrested? Do you think they doubted him at that point? Or were they just afraid?

- Why do you think Jesus said what he did in verse 64? Do you think there was a reason he answered the high priest that way?

Apply

Application Questions

- Have you ever "denied" Jesus in your words or actions? If so, when? How does Peter's denial make you feel?

- What does Jesus' prayer in the garden tell you about the way we should pray? Are you honest with God in your prayers? What (if anything) inhibits you in your prayers?

- What do you think you would have done if you were with Jesus when he got arrested? If you were a follower, do you think your opinion of him would have changed? Why/Why not?

- Have you ever been disappointed in God because of something he did or didn't do for you? How did that affect your relationship with him? Is it affecting your relationship with him right now?

Do

Optional Activity

Over the next week, have your group keep a tally of how many times they show their allegiance to Christ, and how many times they deny they know him (in their words, their actions, or their silence.) They can do this by spending five minutes at the end of the day reflecting on conversations, classes, recreational activities—and writing down any successes or failures. Have them bring their findings to the next group meeting to talk about where they are (and where they'd like to be) in their loyalty to Christ.

QUIET TIME REFLECTIONS

Day 1: Matthew 26:31-35

- What word or verse stands out to you from this passage? Why?

- How does Peter refute Jesus' words to him? How do you think he felt about what Jesus said?

- Spend time thinking about whether you would ever deny Jesus. What would you do if you did?

Day 2: Matthew 26:36-46

- What word or verse stands out to you from this passage? Why?

- What does Jesus want the disciples to do while he is in the garden? Why?

- Spend time praying for friends who are going through tough times. Think about what Jesus says in this passage about how prayer strengthens us.

Day 3: Matthew 26:47-56

- What word or verse stands out to you from this passage? Why?

- How does Jesus show his power in this passage? Why does he willingly submit to his arrest?

- Spend time thinking today about how Jesus shows his strength through submission. How can you do the same?

Day 4: Matthew 26:57-63

- What word or verse stands out to you from this passage? Why?

- How does Jesus exercise self-control in this passage? What could he have done?

- Spend time thinking today about how silence can often be the most powerful response.

Day 5: Matthew 26:64-68

- What word or verse stands out to you from this passage? Why?

- How does Jesus reveal who he is in this passage? What is he alluding to with his words?

- Spend time thinking today about the kind of king Jesus was and the kind he wasn't.

Day 6: Matthew 26:69-75

- What word or verse stands out to you from this passage? Why?

- What happens to Peter after he denies Jesus three times? Have you ever experienced remorse for not standing up for Christ?

- Spend time thinking today about how to be braver in your faith.

Day 7: Matthew 26:31-75

Read through the whole chapter and write out the verse that spoke to you most this week. Meditate on that verse today—and for an extra challenge, memorize it!

28. PILATE'S DILEMMA
Matthew 27:1-26

LEADER'S INSIGHT

Pontius Pilate shows us that when it comes to Jesus Christ, no decision is a decision. And sometimes it's the worst kind of decision there is. The Nicene Creed shows us that Pilate's "non-decision" sentenced him to be remembered forever as the one in charge of Jesus' crucifixion. And his proclamation of innocence in this chapter didn't seem to make a difference in how he was ultimately perceived.

In this chapter, there are two tragic figures. The first is Judas, as we see how he regretfully tries to undo what he's done. The chief priests deny him that opportunity, but instead of running to Jesus for forgiveness and grace, he hangs himself in despair. Judas' inability to forgive himself becomes his ultimate sentence.

Pilate is more complex, as we witness his internal wrestling match for how he will respond to the weight of Jesus' fate. His discomfort is evident as he tries to absolve himself of the responsibility he has. Ultimately he allows Jesus to be sentenced and then tries to step aside and absolve himself of that sentence. He is unsuccessful, as history (and the Nicene Creed) reveal.

Pontius Pilate shows us as believers that when it comes to our relationship with God, we must all take a stand. If we don't, we will ultimately find we are taking one anyway.

Share

- Have you ever felt so guilty about something you couldn't move forward without dealing with it? If so, what did you do?

- What is the toughest decision you've had to make? What made it tough?

- Have you ever tried to blame someone else for something you did, and it backfired? If so, when?

Observe

Observation Questions

- What did Judas try to do in verse 3? How did the chief priests respond in verse 4? What did Judas do then? (verse 5)

- What does Pilate ask Jesus in verse 11? How does Jesus answer? How does Jesus respond to the accusations in verse 12?

- What does Pilate do in verses 15-17? What does verse 18 say about what Pilate knew?

- What did Pilate's wife warn him about? (verse 19) Whom do the people choose to have released? (verse 21) What does Pilate say in verse 24?

Think

Interpretation Questions

- What does verse 3 tell you about Judas? What does verse 5 tell you about him?

- What do you observe about the chief priests in verses 4-7? What did they care about? What didn't they care about?

- Why do you think Jesus answers Pilate the way he does in verse 11? What clues do you get in verses 13-18 about how Pilate feels about Jesus?

- Why do you think Pilate said what he did in verse 24? Do you think he felt innocent? Why/Why not?

Apply

Application Questions

- Based on what you know about Jesus, do you think he would have forgiven Judas if he had repented? Why/why not?

- Have you ever done something you didn't think God could forgive? Do you think there are any sins God doesn't forgive?

- Have you ever felt like Pilate and been afraid to stand up for what you believed? If so, when?

- What is one thing you could do in your life right now to stand strong in what you believe?

Do

Optional Activity

Get a copy of the Nicene Creed (you can look for it on the Internet) and have students look for where Pontius Pilate is mentioned. Discuss whether Pilate ever thought at the moment he allowed Jesus to be sentenced that he would be remembered that way. You can also have your students share if they have said yes or no to Jesus at some point in their lives. Like a marriage proposal, God has offered us a relationship with him, but we have to say yes for the relationship to begin. (Romans 10:9) As Pontius Pilate teaches us, our response to Jesus matters!

QUIET TIME REFLECTIONS

Day 1: Matthew 27:1-4

- What word or verse stands out to you from this passage? Why?

- How does Judas feel about what he did? Have you ever done anything you deeply regret?

- Spend time thinking today about what you would have done at this point if you were Judas.

Day 2: Matthew 27:5-8

- What word or verse stands out to you from this passage? Why?

- What did Judas do with his guilt? What do you think kept him from going back to Jesus?

- Spend time thinking today about how God wants us to go to him with our sin, and not try to deal with the guilt ourselves.

Day 3: Matthew 27:9-10

- What word or phrase stands out to you from this passage? Why?

- How did Judas' actions fulfill prophecy? (See Jeremiah 19, 32.) What does that tell you about God's knowledge of us?

- Spend time thinking today about how God knows your heart better than you do.

Day 4: Matthew 27:11-14

- What word or phrase stands out to you from these verses? Why?

- What does Jesus admit to being in this passage? How does he word his response?

- Spend time thinking today about how Jesus wants us to answer for ourselves who he is.

Day 5: Matthew 27:15-19

- What word or phrase stands out to you from these verses? Why?

- What does Pilate's wife warn him about Jesus? How do you think this made Pilate feel?

- Spend time thinking today about the many ways God communicates with us.

Day 6: Matthew 27:20-26

- What word or phrase stands out to you from these verses? Why?

- How does Pilate try to avoid sentencing Jesus in this chapter? Do you think he is successful?

- Spend time thinking today about how we can't avoid making a decision about Jesus. Pilate shows us no decision is a decision.

Day 7: Matthew 27:1-26

Read through the whole chapter and write out the verse that spoke to you most this week. Meditate on that verse today—and for an extra challenge, memorize it!

29. DEATH ON OUR BEHALF
Matthew 27:27-66

LEADER'S INSIGHT

In this chapter we see how far God was willing to go to prove how much he loves us. He sent his precious son to die an innocent death on our behalf. Like a judge who sentences us for our wrongdoing and then pays the penalty himself, God sent Jesus to be our sacrifice. And the brutal death Jesus experiences in this chapter helps us remember one more time what an amazing act of love this was.

Matthew records in this chapter that when Jesus hung on the cross, people mocked him saying, "He saved others, but he can't save himself!" Yet the irony of that statement is that it was because he was saving others that he refrained from saving himself. How tempting it must have been to call on God to spare him. Instead, he humbly submitted to sparing us.

The stark words Jesus calls out from the cross reveal that for one moment in history, God stood separate from his son. His cry of "Why have you forsaken me?" must have made God cry as he stood at a distance so that we could be absolved. When he finally breathed his last breath, and the earth shook, the people cried out, "Surely this was the Son of God." But it appeared that the Son of God had been defeated.

As he was laid to rest in the tomb, people thought it was the end of the story. But they would soon learn that a better story was just beginning.

That is a great truth to remember when it comes to God.

Share

Warm-Up Questions

- What is the biggest sacrifice someone has made for you? What is the biggest sacrifice you have made for someone else?

- What has been the saddest death you've experienced so far? Why?

- Have you ever had someone give you something so big you could never repay it? If so, what?

Observe

Observation Questions

- What did they do to Jesus before the crucifixion? (verses 28-30) What did they say to him? (verse 29)

- Who carried Jesus' cross? (verse 32) Where did they take him to be crucified? (verse 33) What did they write over his head? (verse 37)

- What do the elders and chief priests say in verses 42-43? What does Jesus say in verse 46? What happened right after that? (verse 50)

- What happened right after Jesus died? (verse 51) Who buried Jesus? (verses 57-60) What did the Pharisees want Pilate to do after that? (verses 62-65)

Think

Interpretation Questions

- Do you find any irony in what the chief priests say in verse 42? If so, what?

- Why do you think Jesus said the words he did in verse 46? What did those words signify?

- What was the significance of what happened in verse 51? (Look back to Old Testament sacrifices to find out.)

- How did the Pharisees' request in verses 63-64 end up working against them? (Think ahead.)

Apply

Application Questions

- Did you notice anything new about the crucifixion story that helps you understand the crucifixion better? If so, what?

- How does what happened on the cross relate to you today? Do Jesus' actions affect you? If so, how?

- What does Jesus' suffering mean to you in your suffering? Does it help you to know that God understands pain?

- Is there any sin you are carrying that you need to claim Jesus' death for? What (if anything) do you need to let God take care of?

Do

Optional Activity

The Walk to the Cross: Rent or borrow *The Passion of the Christ* or the *Jesus* movie and watch the scene of Jesus' excruciating walk to the cross. Have your students watch it prayerfully, silently asking Jesus' forgiveness for any sin they might be carrying. Close your time with a prayer.

QUIET TIME REFLECTIONS

Day 1: Matthew 27:27-31

- What word or verse stands out to you from this passage? Why?

- What did Jesus endure before the crucifixion? How does this passage make you feel?

- Spend time thinking today about how God understands our suffering in Jesus.

Day 2: Matthew 27:32-37

- What word or verse stands out to you from this passage? Why?

- What was written above Jesus' head? Do you think the Pharisees would have wanted this?

- Spend time thinking today about how Jesus is king whether people believe it or not.

Day 3: Matthew 27:38-44

- What word or verse stands out to you from this passage? Why?

- How do the chief priests mock Jesus while he's on the cross? Do you find any irony in the things they say?

- Spend time thinking today about how Jesus didn't save himself so that he could save us.

Day 4: Matthew 27:45-56

- What word or verse stands out to you from this passage? Why?

- What does Jesus cry out to God from the cross? Why did he say those words?

- Spend time thinking today about how Jesus endured separation from God so we could be united with him.

Day 5: Matthew 27:57-61

- What word or verse stands out to you from this passage? Why?

- Who buried Jesus? Why is it important that we know Jesus was buried?

- Spend time thinking today about the days Jesus spent in the tomb and how his followers must have felt.

Day 6: Matthew 27:61-66

- What word or verse stands out to you from this passage? Why?

- How did the chief priests protect Jesus' body from being stolen? How does this refute the theories that try to explain why Jesus' body was missing?

Day 7: Matthew 27:27-66

Read through the whole chapter and write out the verse that spoke to you most this week. Meditate on that verse today—and for an extra challenge, memorize it!

30. RESURRECTION AND NEW LIFE
Matthew 28

LEADER'S INSIGHT

Without the resurrection, Christianity preaches a prophet and a teacher who taught us how to live. With the resurrection, Christianity preaches a Savior who comes to be our Lord. Only one of these has the power to change lives.

The story of the empty tomb opens this final chapter of Matthew, and your students will read once more the story that transforms our faith. Mary and Martha come to see the tomb, and are met by an angel who delivers the famous words: *"He is not here; he has risen just as he said."* As they scurry back to tell the disciples, Jesus meets them on the road, and they clasp his feet and worship him.

While he was alive, they followed. Seeing him resurrected, they worship. Something big has happened to their Lord and their faith. Thinking back, they realize it is just what Jesus said would happen. And now it's their job to tell everyone else. At the end of the chapter, your students will realize it's their job to do that, too.

The mixed reactions and doubts parallel some of the responses we get today when we share the gospel. But Jesus encourages us at the end of the chapter that his power will move through us to bring others to himself. We are not responsible for how people respond. But we are responsible, Jesus says, to get the word out.

Let these words usher forth from our hearts, our souls, and our lives: "He is not here; he has risen!"

Just as he said.

Share

Warm-Up Questions

- What is the biggest surprise you've ever gotten?

- Where do you need new life in an area that feels "dead"?

- Do you think the responsibility for leading others to Jesus is up to God or us? If you believe it's both, which part is God's responsibility and which is ours?

Observe

Observation Questions

- Who went to the tomb first? (verse 1) What happened when they got there? (verses 2-3)

- What did the angel say? (verses 5-7) What did the women do? (verse 8) Who met them along the way? (verse 9)

- Who told the chief priests what happened? (verse 11) What plan did they devise? (verses 12-14)

- What were the reactions when Jesus appeared to the disciples? (verse 17) What did Jesus say to them? (verses 18-20)

Think

Interpretation Questions

- Given the social standing of women in the first century, do you think it was significant that Jesus appeared to two women first? If so, what does it tell you about Jesus?

- How do you think the disciples reacted to the women's story? (Look at Luke 24:11 for clues.)

- Why do you think the chief priests created a different story about what happened? (verse 12) How do you think they felt after the guards' report?

- Why do you think some doubted when they saw the resurrected Jesus? (verse 17) Do you think his appearance was different? Why did others worship him when they saw him?

Apply

- How do you picture angels based on the accounts you've read (like this one)? Have you ever experienced anything that seemed like an angel was present?

- Have you ever doubted the resurrection or wondered if it really happened? How important do you think the resurrection is to our faith? (See 1 Corinthians 15:14.)

- How have you seen the Great Commission lived out since Jesus spoke it in this chapter?

- What have you personally done to fulfill the Great Commission? Do you find it easy or hard to share your faith?

Do

Optional Activity

"Tell the Story." Give your students two minutes each to tell the story of who Jesus was and why he came. Give them some time to write down or think through their thoughts, and then share how they would tell the story of Jesus to someone who didn't know it. Have your group vote on who tells it best, and give a prize to the winner. This is a great exercise for students to learn how to highlight the important parts of the Gospel, and be equipped to share it with someone to fulfill the Great Commission.

QUIET TIME REFLECTIONS

Day 1: Matthew 28:1-4

- What word or verse stands out to you from this passage? Why?

- How did the guards react to the angel? What does that tell you about the angel's appearance?

- Spend time thinking today about how you picture angels. Why do you think people are afraid of them?

Day 2: Matthew 28:5-7

- What word or phrase stands out to you from these verses? Why?

- What did the angel tell the two women? How do you think they felt?

- Spend time today thinking about how you would have felt if you were with the women at the tomb.

Day 3: Matthew 28:8-10

- What word or phrase stands out to you from these verses? Why?

- How do the women respond to Jesus when they see him? What would you have done?

- Spend time thinking today about what it means to worship Jesus. Do you have to be in church to do it?

Day 4: Matthew 28:11-15

- What word or phrase stands out to you from these verses? Why?

- What story did the chief priests make up about Jesus' body being gone?

- Spend time thinking today about the many theories that

have been given to explain the resurrection. Which do you think is most believable?

Day 5: Matthew 28:16-17

- What word or phrase stands out to you from these verses? Why?

- What two reactions did the disciples have when they saw Jesus? Which do you think you would have had?

- Spend time thinking today about any doubts you have about Jesus. What can you do about them?

Day 6: Matthew 28:18-20

- What word or phrase stands out to you from these verses? Why?

- What words does Jesus leave us with? What (if anything) have you done to fulfill the Great Commission?

- Spend time thinking today of one person you could share the good news with. Pray for the courage to do it!

Day 7: Matthew 28

Read through the whole chapter and write out the verse that spoke to you most this week. Meditate on that verse today—and for an extra challenge, memorize it!